SALT OF THE EARTH

Study on
Setting the Captives Free,
Salt of the Earth,
Parables, and
John the Baptist

by H.M. Schuldt

"Salt is good,
but if the salt loses its saltiness,
with what will you season it?
Have salt among yourselves,
and be at peace with one another."

Jesus Christ
(Mark 9:50 ESV)

TABLE OF CONTENTS

Group Directions

Session Guidelines

Small Group Guidelines

Session Overview

GROUP DIRECTIONS

Each Session – Suggested format is as follows:

5 minutes - Welcome, name tags, sit in sanctuary or living room.
10-15 minutes - Praise and worship music for all to sing to the Lord, lyrics provided, and call upon His name.
Praise songs suggested include:
Blessed Be the Name of the Lord (Strong Tower)
Refiner's Fire
Cornerstone
Holy Forever

10 minutes - Salvation testimony from one person – speak to everyone in the large group. Leaders: Photocopy Session Three, Day 1, Number 2, "Share Your Salvation Testimony," ask people to fill it out, and turn it in before the next week.

1 hour – Small groups. Split up into small groups of 3-8 people in separate locations with a designated facilitator in each group. See Small Group Guidelines.

TOTAL: 90 minutes
Optional: Additional 20-minute lesson from a spirit-filled Bible Teacher

Large Group Leader - A leader of the large group will coordinate and pray for small groups with 3-8 people in each group. The leader will provide a private space for each small group to meet, discuss, and pray. The leader will unlock doors or find someone responsible to unlock them.
Pray for your large group leaders.

Small Group Facilitator - A small group facilitator will prepare ahead of time by praying for the people in their group. The facilitator does not need to teach. Let the Holy Spirit teach, convict, comfort, and guide. A table is preferred but not necessary. Someone needs to provide chairs. The small group facilitator can provide a table runner, tissue, pens, a spiral notebook for people to write down prayers, and a simple, nonallergenic centerpiece if possible. Pray for your small group facilitator and mentors.

SESSION GUIDELINES

Session One – In the small group, spend 5 minutes introducing your name, how long you've lived in the area, and where you grew up. Each week, spend 45 minutes to 1 hour on the questions and answers. Go around one at a time for each person to read a question and answer. During the hour, pass around a spiral notebook and pen for optional written prayers. Spend the last 15 minutes calling on the name of the Lord and praying out loud. For example, have each person pray for the person on their left.

      Chapter One Date(s): _____

Session Two – In the small group, spend 5 minutes on when you first heard about Jesus as the Savior, Jesus as God, and/or surrender to Jesus as your Lord and Savior. Spend 45 minutes to 1 hour on the questions and answers in chapter two. Each person will pray for the person on their right.

      Chapter Two Date(s): _____

Session Three – Encourage everyone to pray for the salvation of someone at the end of small group time. Spend 45 minutes to 1 hour on the questions and answers in chapter three. Spend the last 15 minutes in prayer. Pray for salvation, revival, and prodigals to repent from sin and return to the Lord.

      Chapter Three Date(s): _____

Session Four – Encourage everyone to praise God for His character and thank Him for his wonderful work. Spend 45 minutes to 1 hour on the questions and answers in chapter four. Pass the prayer notebook around. Spend the last 15 minutes in prayer.

      Chapter Four Date(s): _____

Pray for people in your small group.

SMALL GROUP GUIDELINES

1. **LOVE** - Love is patient. Love is kind. Encourage everyone to show the fruit of the Spirit in the small group (See Galatians 5:22-23).

2. **VALUE** - Do not force anyone to discuss personal matters. Value each person (See Genesis 1:27, Imago Dei).

3. **USE A PEN** - Write in this study guidebook. Make sure you have a pen that works.

4. **MENTORS** - Honor all seasoned mentors. Ask them to facilitate the group one week if they want to. Ask them to open or close in prayer. Take turns praying.

5. **GIVE OPTIONS** - No homework is necessary, but people are welcome to go over questions each day during the week and add any additional notes.

6. **FOUR WEEKS OR MORE** - Consider doing this study over four to eight sessions to cover everything. You might discuss Days 1-2 in small group. Then discuss Days 3-5 the next time you get together, depending if you want to chat for one hour, ninety minutes, or two hours, etc.

7. **STICK TO TRUTH** - No false teaching. No heresies. Agree to disagree peacefully on minor interpretation differences. God's Word has no errors.

8. **HONOR THE AUTHORS of the BIBLE as Inspired by the Holy Spirit** - Discuss the author's meaning of Scripture. Praise God for his character and work. Thank God for the Bible.

9. **PRAY** - Set a timer to begin and end prayer. A timer helps the leader stay on time. Always allow time for prayer. Stay flexible to pray immediately. Jesus said, "My house shall be called a house of prayer." (See Matthew 21:13)

10. **BE ON TIME** – Start on time. Close on time. Respect the time other people are putting into this study. Thank your leaders, facilitators, mentors, and everyone who attends.

SESSION ONE OVERVIEW
Setting the Captives Free

Ministry of Jesus: Inner Healing

DAY 1 – Isaiah's Prophecy
1. Anointing
2. Humble and Meek
3. Brokenhearted
4. Captives
5. Blindness
6. New Blessings from Heaven
7. Fulfilled Prophecy

DAY 2 – Spirit of the Lord
1. Day of Vengeance
2. Wilderness
3. Divine Power
4. Mountaintop

DAY 3 – First Impressions
1. God Sees
2. Identity of Jesus
3. Belief and Unbelief
4. Miracle Worker
5. Cleaning Our Heart
6. Elijah and Elisha
7. Taking Instructions

DAY 4 – Shake Off the Dust
1. Moving Right Along
2. Escape Route
3. Safe From Danger
4. Comfort From Danger

DAY 5 – Armor of God
Personal Application

DAY 6 – Rest

DAY 7 –Corporate Worship

Praise Songs

The name of the LORD is a strong tower

I will call upon the Lord who is worthy to be praised

House of Miracles

Praise by Brandon Lake, Chris Brown, and Chandler Moore

SESSION TWO OVERVIEW
Salt of the Earth

You Shall be Salted with Fire

DAY 1 – Miracles
1. Water into Wine
2. Official's Son's Illness
3. Unclean Spirit
4. Speak the Good News
5. Catching Fish
6. Healing a Leper
7. Paralyzed Man
8. Withered Hand
9. No Miracle

DAY 2 – Beatitudes
1. We Need God
2. Mourning a Loss
3. Humble and Strong
4. Hunger and Thirst
5. Merciful
6. Pure in Heart
7. Peacemakers
8. Stand Up for Righteousness

DAY 3 – Get Right with God
1. Sin Offering
2. Covenant of Salt
3. Davidic Covenant
4. Eternal Covenant
5. Faithful to Keep Promises
6. Jesus! Have Mercy on Me!
7. Pay Close Attention

DAY 4 – God Provides Salt
1. Required in the Temple
2. Salty Wisdom
3. Salty Works
4. Salty Speech
5. Salty Life
6. Salty Flavor

DAY 5 – Five Purposes of Salt
1. Warning
2. Five Purposes
3. Five Ways to be Salty
4. Boast in the Lord
5. Judge Behavior
6. Nourish Your Soul

DAY 6 – Armor of God
Personal Application

DAY 7 – Rest and Corporate Worship

Praise Songs

Refiner's Fire

I Speak Jesus

SESSION THREE OVERVIEW

Five More Parables of Jesus

DAY 1 – Let Your Light Shine
1. Show Good Work
2. Share your Salvation Testimony
3. Walk in Truth
4. Truth Sets us Free from Falsehood
5. Live a Blameless Life
6. Hold Fast to the Word of Life
7. Redeemed People
8. City on a Hill
9. Divine Light

DAY 2 – Spec and Log
1. Logs in the Eye
2. Learn Divine Secrets
3. Judge Rebellious Behavior
4. Divine Wrath
5. Praise God for His Good Work
6. Good Work People Do
7. Four Tips for Judging
8. Govern People Well
9. Solomon's Palace

DAY 3 – Two Gates (Narrow and Wide Gates)
1. Two Options
2. Three Options
3. Wickedness Before the World Flood
4. Coming of the Son of Man
5. Human Heart
6. Wide Road of Destruction
7. Narrow Path of Life
8. Wash Your Robe
9. Abundant Life

DAY 4 – House on a Rock
1. Meaning of House on a Rock
2. Diligent Work
3. Cornerstone
4. Waking Up
5. Divine Words of Jesus
6. Great Storm at Sea
7. Remain Steadfast
8. Prepare for Jesus to Return

DAY 5 – New Wine
1. Call on the Name of the Lord
2. Everlasting Covenant
3. Melchizedek
4. Abraham Built Altars
5. Levite Priests
6. Samuel the Prophet
7. Elijah's Contest
8. Jesus, the Great High Priest
9. New Covenant
10. New Wine, the New Way

DAY 6 – Armor of God Personal Application

DAY 7 – Rest and Corporate Worship

Praise Songs

Cornerstone

The Lord's Prayer

SESSION FOUR OVERVIEW

John the Baptist

DAY 1 – Ministry of John the Baptist
1. Gabriel Prophesied to Zechariah
2. Prepare the Way
3. Turn Away from Ungodly Behavior
4. Power from Jesus Christ
5. Voice from Heaven
6. Wheat and Chaff Parable

DAY 2 – Old Testament Washings
1. Consecration at Mount Sinai
2. Bronze Basin
3. Priestly Purification
4. Steadfast Love
5. Water Baptism

DAY 3 – John, a Friend of the Bridegroom
1. Increase and Decrease
2. Lead Them to Jesus
3. Give Them Assurance
4. Bring Others to Jesus
5. John's Answer to Isaac
6. Glory to the Lamb

DAY 4 – Water Baptism & Fire Baptism
1. Believe Jesus
2. The Mighty One
3. Empowered for Kingdom Work
4. Joel's Prophecy Fulfilled
5. Washing from the Holy Spirit
6. Empowered for a Purpose
7. New Life in Christ

DAY 5 – Kingdom of Heaven on Earth
1. Son the Living God
2. Possibly or Certainly
3. Paul, a Faithful Witness
4. Get Baptized
5. Gifts for Kingdom Work
6. Malachi's Prophecy

DAY 6 – Armor of God Personal Application

DAY 7 – Rest and Corporate Worship

Praise Songs

Holy Forever

Chapter 1

SETTING THE CAPTIVES FREE

(Luke 4:14-30)

The Last Supper
Leonardo da Vinci, c. 1495

Ministry of Jesus: Inner Healing

Then the angel showed me the river of the water of life,
bright as crystal, flowing from the throne of God
and of the Lamb
through the middle of the street of the city,
also, on either side of the river,
the tree of life with its twelve kinds of fruit,
yielding its fruit each month.
The leaves of the tree were for
the healing of the nations.
Revelation 22:1-2

At the beginning of Jesus' 3-year ministry, Jesus went throughout Galilee, taught in synagogues, proclaimed good news of the divine kingdom on earth, and healed every disease. News about Jesus spread throughout Galilee, the whole countryside, and all over Syria.

One Sabbath day, Jesus was in his hometown synagogue when He stood up to read Scripture. He read a section from the book of Isaiah where the prophet, Isaiah, had prophesied the Holy Spirit would anoint the future Messiah.

Luke recorded the beginning of Jesus's ministry in Luke 4:14-30. The teaching of Jesus in the synagogue that day included the following five parts:

- Prophecy Fulfilled (verses 14-21)
- Hometown prophets (22-24)
- The story of Elijah in Zarephath (25-26)
- Elisha's instructions to Naaman (27)
- Jesus walked away from an angry crowd (28-30)

Read Luke 4:14-21 (ESV) below.

And Jesus returned in the power of the Spirit to Galilee, and a report about him went out through all the surrounding country. And he taught in their synagogues, being glorified by all.

And he came to Nazareth, where he had been brought up. And as was his custom, he went to the synagogue on the Sabbath day, and he stood up to read. And the scroll of the prophet Isaiah was given to him. He unrolled the scroll and found the place where it was written,

"The Spirit of the Lord is upon me, because he has anointed me to proclaim good news to the poor. He has sent me to proclaim liberty to the captives and recovering of sight to the blind, to set at liberty those who are oppressed, to proclaim the year of the Lord's favor."

And he rolled up the scroll and gave it back to the attendant and sat down. And the eyes of all in the synagogue were fixed on him. And he began to say to them, "Today this Scripture has been fulfilled in your hearing."

Session One: Setting the Captives Free

A scroll was given to Jesus for him to read from the book of Isaiah. It was a short and powerful reading that led to a surprise ending. Jesus read from Isaiah chapter 61, verses 1-2, but he only read the first part of verse 2. Below, notice the underlined portion that Jesus read out loud.

Read Isaiah 61:1-2 (ESV) below.

(Verse 1) *The Spirit of the Lord GOD* (Adonai Yahweh) *is upon me because the LORD* (Yahweh) *has anointed me to bring (proclaim) good news (good tidings) to the poor (humble and meek). He has sent me to bind up (heal) the brokenhearted, to proclaim liberty (forgiveness) to the captives (oppressed), and the opening of the prison to those who are bound (blind),* (Verse 2) *to proclaim the year of the LORD's favor* (Yahweh's)… and the day of vengeance of our God, to comfort all who mourn…

The book of Isaiah was written about 700 years before Jesus.

List five acts of kindness in the ministry of Jesus, based on Isaiah 61:1-2:

1.

2.

3.

4.

5.

Jesus read Isaiah 61:1-2 accurately from a Hebrew scroll. He spoke most likely in Aramaic or Hebrew. The ministry of Jesus is spiritual, but it can also be physical. Dr. Luke recorded the ministry of Jesus without any error in Luke 4:18-19. Scholars are welcome to use the original Hebrew Old Testament manuscript and the original Greek New Testament manuscript to compare Isaiah 6:1-2 with the fulfilled ministry of Jesus in Luke 4:18-19. Use the chart below to confirm fulfillment.

🔍 Let's compare
Isa.61:1-2 & Lk. 4:18-19
(ESV)

Isaiah 61:1-2	Luke 4:18-19
The Spirit of the Lord GOD is upon me because the LORD has anointed me ☑	The Spirit of the LORD is upon me because He has anointed me
to bring good news (good tidings) to the poor (humble & meek). ☑	to proclaim good news to the poor.
He has sent me to bind up (heal) the brokenhearted,	He has sent me to proclaim liberty to the captives, ☑
to proclaim liberty to the captives,	and recovering of sight to the blind, ☑
and the opening of the prison to those who are bound (blind);	to set at liberty those who are oppressed ☑
to proclaim the year of the LORD's favor... ☑	to proclaim the year of the LORD's favor...

MINISTRY OF JESUS:
- Bring good news to those who know they need God.
- Release people from the captivity of sin, addiction, gluttony, etc.
- Heal people from blindness of unbelief, disease, and sickness.
- Set people free from brokenness, oppression, unforgiveness, and abuse. Deliver people from evil, Satan, destruction, and hate.

Dear Heavenly Father, thank you for the ministry of Jesus. You deliver us from captivity, blindness, and oppression. You help us hear good news, experience freedom, and break free from darkness. Heal our broken heart. All praise to You, God! In Jesus name, Amen.

DAY 1 – Isaiah's Prophecy

Jesus began reading from the book of Isaiah, chapter 61. It is the beginning of Jesus's 3-year ministry as recorded in the book of Luke.

(For Leaders: In your small group, let people know what version of the Bible you are using. It is fine to read from an ESV, NASB, NLT, NKJV, or the older NIV. Do not require everyone to read your version. It is easier to follow along if everyone has the same version, but let people use the version they are comfortable with. Heretical versions are not allowed. Ask a mentor or a Bible student to go to the Greek New Testament manuscript or Hebrew Old Testament manuscript to clarify any differences in interpretation between versions.)

Describe seven marvelous things about the coming Messiah, prophesied by Isaiah about 700 years earlier.

1. **Anointing** - Who will anoint the Messiah?

2. **Humble** - What will the Messiah proclaim to the humble and meek?

3. **Brokenhearted** - What will the Messiah do to the brokenhearted?

4. **Captives** - What will the Messiah proclaim to the captives?

5. **Blindness** - What will the Messiah do to the blind?

6. **New Blessings from Heaven** –What year will the Messiah proclaim?

7. **Fulfilled Prophecy** - Why did Jesus roll up the scroll in the middle of verse two?

And he (Jesus) began to say to them, "Today this Scripture has been fulfilled in your hearing."

(Luke 4:21)

Jesus proclaims liberty to the captives by freeing people from the bondage of corruption. He provides freedom to people so they can love and serve God. Jesus has authority to forgive sins, give power over sin, and give eternal life to all who receive him by faith as his or her personal Savior. (See John 3:16, Romans 8:21, Galatians 5:13, 1 Peter 2:16)

Dear Lord God Almighty, I want to learn more about the true ministry of Jesus. Help me understand how Jesus healed the brokenhearted and set the captives free. Help me and my family hear – with accurate meaning - the teachings of Jesus. Help us share the good news Jesus taught to those who are humble. Let us escape from danger like Jesus did. Help us know You and have a personal relationship with You. Help us persevere various challenges we are going through. Cleanse us from all unrighteousness by the power of your Holy Spirit fire. I want to know You and love You with all my heart. Be glorified in our life now and forevermore. Let your will be done. In Jesus name, Amen.

DAY 2 – Spirit of the Lord

Jesus read verse one and only the first half of verse two from Isaiah 61:1-2. Then He rolled up the scroll and gave it back to the attendant and sat down (See Luke 4:20). The reason why Jesus stopped reading where he did is because His ministry fulfills the following:

- He proclaims good news
- Heals the brokenhearted
- Gives sight to the blind
- Delivers the oppressed
- Proclaims the year of the Lord's favor

1. **Day of Vengeance** - What part of Isaiah 61:2 did Jesus not read? Why do you think Jesus did not read it?

2. **The Wilderness** - Just before Jesus gave this sermon, where did the Spirit lead him? For how long? For what reason? Read Luke 4:1 below.

And Jesus, full of the Holy Spirit, returned from the Jordan and was led by the Spirit in the wilderness for forty days, being tempted by the devil.
(Luke 4:1)

3. **Divine Power** - The Holy Spirit of God gives power to Jesus.
Read Luke 4:14 below.

> *And Jesus returned in the power of the Spirit to Galilee, and a report about him went out through all the surrounding country.*
> (Luke 4:14)

Who do we get power from? Read Acts 1:8 below.

> *But you will receive power when the Holy Spirit has come upon you, and you will be my witnesses in Jerusalem and in all Judea and Samaria, and to the end of the earth.*
> (Acts 1:8)

What kind of power does the Holy Spirit give?

> *The Spirit of the LORD shall rest upon him,*
> *the Spirit of wisdom and understanding,*
> *the Spirit of counsel and might,*
> *the Spirit of knowledge and the fear of the LORD.*
> (Isaiah 11:2)

Pray for five of your neighbors to hear the good news message that God gives eternal life to all who believe in Jesus Christ (See John 3:16). Write their first name below and pray for their salvation.
If they are already saved, pray for their sanctification.

4. **Mountaintop Experience** - Jesus took Peter and John up on a mountain to pray. Peter and John were instructed to do something very important.

What did a voice in a cloud instruct Peter and John to do?

> *And a voice came out of the cloud, saying, "This is my Son, my Chosen One; listen to him!"*
> (Luke 9:35)

What did the voice say about the nature of Jesus?

> *He was still speaking when, behold, a bright cloud overshadowed them, and a voice from the cloud said, "This is my beloved Son, with whom I am well pleased; listen to him."*
> (Matthew 17:5)

> Dear Heavenly Father,
> help us listen to Jesus, the Word of God.
> Help us to know Jesus as the Son of God.
> Like John the disciple, help us know Jesus,
> the Word who became flesh and dwelt among us.
> Amen.

> *And the Word (Logos) became flesh and dwelt among us, and we have seen his glory, glory as of the only Son from the Father (Patros), full of grace and truth.*
> (John 1:14)

DAY 3 – First Impressions

After reading from Isaiah, people spoke well of Jesus and wondered where he came from. Scripture says *all people spoke well of him,* and people wondered what family he had come from. The first impression of Jesus was that the people were impressed. While first impressions can be important, a first impression is really a judgment, either an accurate or inaccurate judgment. According to statistics, people tend to make the following judgments on appearance when hiring, electing an official, or selecting a church to attend:

OBSERVATION	FIRST IMPRESSION
Physical beauty	Healthy/Impressed
Apparel	Success/Approve
Eloquent Speech	Competent/Marvel
Practical shoes	Agreeable/Prudent
Stylish shoes	Wealthy/Cool

You've probably heard the saying, "Don't judge a book by its cover." Yet, we often develop opinions by how a person looks or what a person says. Think about a time when you were going through a difficult situation. You might have explained it to someone, but they did not completely understand what you were going through. You might have reached out to someone, hoping to find some compassion, but the person was unable to empathize or give you any hope. The good news is that God always knows what you are going through. He always cares. He is always faithful to help us when we call on Him. He always gives us hope.

1. **God Sees the Real You** - What does God pay attention to when He looks at a person? Read 1 Samuel 16:7 below.

But the LORD said to Samuel, "Do not consider his appearance or height, for I have rejected him; the LORD does not see as man does. For man sees the outward appearance, but the LORD sees the heart.

Read Luke 4:20-22 below.

And he rolled up the scroll and gave it back to the attendant and sat down. And the eyes of all in the synagogue were fixed on him. And he began to say to them, "Today this Scripture has been fulfilled in your hearing." And all spoke well of him and marveled at the gracious words that were coming from his mouth. And they said, "Is not this Joseph's son?"

JUST FOR FUN: Below, note any first impressions that you think are important for a church leader.

- o   The person's parents or family situation

- o   The person's appearance

- o   What the person says

- o   The person's education

- o   Is this person humble?
- o   Is this person living a holy life?
- o   Does this person love Jesus?
- o   Is this person doing kingdom work?
- o   Does this person have a heart for Jesus to heal the brokenhearted?
- o   Does this person extend mercy to people?
- o   Is this person providing food to anyone?

- o   List any other important qualities for a church leader.

2. **Identity of Jesus** - Jesus was identified as the "son of Joseph." Below, notice how some of the people in the synagogue identified Jesus. Their downfall was that they limited the identity of Jesus to his parents, siblings, and work as a carpenter. Jesus is much more than just the son of Mary or a carpenter. In a similar way, you are much more than just a son, daughter, wife, brother, or sister. Dear Lord, help us know the identity of Jesus. Amen.

Read Mark's recorded testimony below:
And on the Sabbath, he (Jesus) began to teach in the synagogue, and many who heard him were astonished, saying, "Where did this man get these things? What is the wisdom given to him? How are such mighty works done by his hands? Is not this the carpenter, the son of Mary and brother of James and Joseph and Judas and Simon? And are not his sisters here with us?" And they took offense at him. (Mark 6:2-3)

How do you identify Jesus? Tell someone you love that Jesus is... the Savior of the world.
- Almighty One (Rev. 1:8)
- Alpha and Omega (Rev. 22:13)
- Advocate (1 John 2:1)
- All Authority (Matt. 28:18)
- Bread of Life (John 6:35)
- Beloved Son of God (Matt. 3:17)
- Chief Cornerstone (Ps. 118:22)
- Deliverer (1 Thess. 1:10)
- Good Shepherd (John 10:11)
- Great High Priest (Heb. 4:14)
- Head of the Church (Eph. 1:22)
- I AM (John 8:58)
- Immanuel (Is. 7:14)
- Judge (Acts 10:42)
- King of Kings (Rev. 17:14)
- Lamb of God (John 1:29)
- Light of the World (John 8:12)
- Messiah (John 1:41)
- Prophet (Mark 6:4)
- Resurrection (John 11:25)
- Savior of the world (Luke 2:11)
- The Way, Truth, and Life (John 14:6)
- The Word of God (John 1:1)

3. **Belief and Unbelief** - Even though some people took offense at Jesus, Jesus continued to teach in the villages.

As soon as new information is given, a listener might come to the wrong conclusion. They might discern inaccurately, make false accusations, get jealous, or simply want to argue, rebel, hate, or hurl insults. In the verses below, find reasons why some people were taking offense.

What is the reason why Jesus could do no mighty work with those particular people?

And he could do no mighty work there, except that he laid his hands on a few sick people and healed them. And he marveled because of their unbelief. And he went about among the villages teaching. (Mark 6:5-6)

> Dear Lord God Almighty,
> I believe in YOU.
> Help my unbelief!
> Amen.

What kind of division occurred at that time?

There was again a division among the Jews because of these words. Many of them said, "He has a demon, and is insane; why listen to him?" Others said, "These are not the words of one who is oppressed by a demon. Can a demon open the eyes of the blind?" (John 10:19-21)

> Jesus said,
> *"And blessed is the one who is not offended by me."*
> Matthew 11:6

> I am not offended by Jesus.
> Thus, I am blessed.

4. **Miracle Worker** - The proverb, "Physician, heal yourself," is not found in the Old Testament. Rather, it was floating around in the culture as a way to encourage doctors to take good care of their own health; or in this case, to not neglect the health of hometown folks. It could also be an insult to point out hypocrisy in a doctor who couldn't heal himself while the doctor attempted to heal others. A similar saying can be found in a Greek tragedy, *Prometheus Bound*, circa 479 BC.

> "Like an unskilled doctor, fallen ill, you lose heart and cannot discover by which remedies to cure your own disease."

However, Jesus was already healthy. Jesus knew the people were demanding miracles from a place of disrespect, contempt, and scorn. They wanted a miracle without valuing the one who gives miracles. They wanted a healing without honoring the one who heals.

Read Luke 4:23-24 below.

> *And he (Jesus) said to them, "Doubtless you will quote to me this proverb, 'Physician, heal yourself.' What we have heard you did at Capernaum, do here in your hometown as well." And he said, "Truly, I say to you, no prophet is acceptable in his hometown."*

Simply put, we are all called to love God more than God's miracles.

Decide which one you choose this day to love more:

Healing or	♡ God the Healer
Saved from danger or	♡ God the Savior
Blessings Given or	♡ God who Gives
Provisions or	♡ God who Provides
Creation or	♡ God the Creator
Miracles or	♡ God the Miracle Worker

5. **Cleaning Our Heart** - Jesus knew the people wanted him to perform a miracle like he did in Capernaum, but Jesus also knew the condition of their darkened hearts, even though they "spoke well of him."

   The following five verses explain how to clean our *heart*. The biblical meaning of *heart* relates to an anthropological description of the inner person. A person's heart is figurative for the emotional and intellectual connection, including desires, intentions, and morals.

   a. Generally speaking, how do we need to clean our hearts?
      Read John 15:3 below.

      Already you are clean because of the word that I have spoken to you.

   b. More specifically, how can we make sure we clean our hearts?
      Read Hebrews 10:22 below.

      ...let us draw near with a true heart in full assurance of faith, with our hearts sprinkled clean from an evil conscience and our bodies washed with pure water.

c. Who does the actual cleaning? Read Titus 3:5 below.

He saved us, not because of works done by us in righteousness, but according to his own mercy, by the washing of regeneration and renewal of the Holy Spirit.

d. How do we overcome a dark heart? Read Revelation 12:11 below.

And they have conquered him by the blood of the Lamb and by the word of their testimony, for they loved not their lives even unto death.

e. What is happening when we let God clean our heart?
    Read Romans 12:2 below.

Do not be conformed to this world, but be transformed by the renewal of your mind, that by testing you may discern what is the will of God, what is good and acceptable and perfect.

6. **Work of Elijah and Elisha** - Jesus referred to the following two stories of Elijah and Elisha. These two prophets show us their type of obedient work, reaching out to people in another city.

- Elijah's work in Sidon
- Elisha's call to help Naaman the Syrian

Read Luke 4:25-27 below.

But in truth, I tell you, there were many widows in Israel in the days of Elijah, when the heavens were shut up three years and six months, and a great famine came over all the land, and Elijah was sent to none of them but only to Zarephath, in the land of Sidon, to a woman who was a widow. And there were many lepers in Israel in the time of the prophet Elisha, and none of them was cleansed, but only Naaman the Syrian.

What did the Lord God instruct Elijah to do?
(See 1 Kings 17:8-16) Check all that apply.

- o Go to Zarephath, a small Phoenician town in the land of Sidon; also called Sarepta in the New Testament. Today, it is called Surafend (17:9).
- o Dwell in Zarephath (17:9).
- o Be fed by a widow. (17:9)
- o Prophesy, "The jar of flour shall not be spent, and the jug of oil shall not be empty, until the day that the Lord sends rain upon the earth" (17:14-16)

7. **Taking Instructions** - What did Elisha instruct/invite Naaman to do?
(See 2 Kings 5:8-14) Check all that apply.

   ○ Elisha invited Naaman to visit him at his house (5:8).
   ○ Know that there is a prophet in Israel (5:8).
   ○ Wash in the Jordan seven times (5:10-14).
   ○ Be healed by washing seven times, consistently.

Maybe you already take a shower seven days in a row. Consider what other kind of good habits you might need to do seven days in a row.

JUST FOR FUN: Consider making these a good habit:

Create a morning ritual.
Prioritize tasks with the biggest impact.
Read, learn, apply.
Single tasking (avoid attention deficit multitasking).
Appreciate more.
Surround yourself with positive, mindful people.
Make time for exercise and work.
Master the art of listening.
Do a social media detox.
Invest in self-care with protein, enough sleep, and godly fun.

Here are tips to develop good habits:

Work on your daily habits "system/process" (not setting goals).
Decide who you want to become, not what you want to achieve.
Make your desired habits obvious.
Make them attractive.
Make them easy.
Make them satisfying.
Update your environment.

Lord Jesus, come and help us develop good habits that please You.

DAY 4 – Shake Off the Dust

When Jesus read verses from Isaiah 61, he knew that darkness was in the hearts of the people who were there listening to him in his hometown. Their dark heart included unbelief and inaccurate discernment about the nature of Jesus. Until our soul gets to heaven and we receive our immortal bodies, we will also encounter people on earth who have not dealt with their unbelief and people who have not dealt with their lack of discernment about the divine nature of Jesus.

1. **Moving Right Along** - How did Jesus respond to a group's unbelief when Jesus mentioned both Elijah and Elisha were called by God to help people in other cities?

> *When they heard these things, all in the synagogue were filled with wrath. And they rose up and drove him out of the town and brought him to the brow of the hill on which their town was built, so that they could throw him down the cliff. But passing through their midst, he went away.*
>
> - Luke 4:28-30

Jesus did not let a group's unbelief stop him from fulfilling prophecy. At times, we need to shake the dust off, leave, move on, and speak the good news Gospel message to other people who are willing to listen and learn.

Read Matthew 10:14 below.

> *And if anyone will not welcome you or heed your words, shake the dust off your feet when you leave that home or town. Truly I tell you, it will be more bearable for Sodom and Gomorrah on the day of judgment than for that town.*

> Pray for whoever speaks against you, whoever is not welcoming you, or whoever is not listening to your salvation testimony. Ask God if it is time to move right along. Jesus instructs us to pray for those who mistreat us, love them, and even bless them (Luke 6:27-28).

2. **Escape Route** - Jesus found an escape route more than once.
   Read John 8:58-59 below.

   Jesus said to them (the Pharisees), "Truly, truly, I say to you, before Abraham was, I am." So they picked up stones to throw at him, but Jesus hid himself and went out of the temple.

   Jesus escaped angry Pharisees time and time again. Jesus knew the Jewish Sanhedrin had the authority to try a criminal case, but they did not have Roman authority to carry out the death penalty. This is why the head priests later took Jesus to Pilate for death by Roman crucifixion.

   During the 3-year ministry of Jesus Christ, was it lawful for Jews to put anyone to death? Read John 18:31-32 below.

   Pilate said to them, "Take him yourselves and judge him by your own law." The Jews said to him, "It is not lawful for us to put anyone to death." This was to fulfill the word that Jesus had spoken to show by what kind of death he was going to die.

3. **Safe From Danger** – Even though the Pharisees wanted to kill him, Jesus affirmed to the Pharisees that he is the Son of God. He explained to them that he is doing divine work, and he was consecrated (declared sacred) by the Father God. He further explained that the Father God is in him, and he is in the Father God. (See John 10:22-42). Jesus had to escape from them again.

   Read John 10:39 below.

   Again, they sought to arrest him (Jesus), but he escaped from their hands.

   Where did Jesus escape to? Read John 10:40 below.

   He (Jesus) went away again across the Jordan to the place where John had been baptizing at first, and there he remained.

   Meditate on Psalm 32:7 - *You (God) are a hiding place for me; you preserve me from trouble; you surround me with shouts of deliverance. Selah.*

4. **Comfort From Heaven** - When we face difficult situations, God can comfort us, give us strength, and help us comfort others who are struggling.

   Find at least one verse that is comforting and encouraging.
   Meditate on it.

   a. Select a verse from Psalm 27.

   > *The LORD is my light and my salvation; whom shall I fear?*
   > *The LORD is the stronghold of my life; of whom shall I be*
   > *afraid?*
   > (Psalm 27:1)

   b. Select a verse from Psalm 40.

   > *I waited patiently for the LORD; he inclined to me and heard*
   > *my cry.*
   > (Psalm 40:1)

   c. Meditate on 2 Corinthians 1:3-4 and let it be your prayer.

   > *Blessed be the God and Father of our Lord Jesus Christ, the*
   > *Father of mercies and God of all comfort, who comforts us*
   > *in all our affliction, so that we may be able to comfort those*
   > *who are in any affliction, with the comfort with which we*
   > *ourselves are comforted by God.*

   d. Sing the praise song from Proverbs 18:10.

   Sing: Blessed Be the Name of the Lord (Strong Tower)

   > *The name of the LORD is a strong tower;*
   > *the righteous run into it and they are safe.*

DAY 5 – Put on the whole Armor of God

PERSONAL APPLICATION - The sword of the Spirit is the Word of God. We are to use the Word of God, not misuse it (See Ephesians 6:10-20). The following verses are suggestions. Write down whatever verses the Holy Spirit brings to your mind. Keep in mind, some people are comfortable sharing personal things, but other people are not.

1. In Luke 4:14-30, is there a sin to avoid? If so, what is it? (Matthew 5:21-22)

2. Is there a divine promise to trust? If so, what is it? (Luke 4:21)

3. Is there a command to obey? If so, what is it? (Gal. 5:16-21)

4. What does this passage say about God's character, his nature, or his work? (1 Cor. 1:9, Heb. 10:23)

5. What does this passage say about mankind? (1 Peter 3:9-12)

6. Is there an example to follow?
   (Luke 4:30, 1 Cor. 10:13)

7. How can I respond in prayer?
   (Psalm 18)

8. What verse can I meditate on?
   (Psalm 18:29)

9. How can I use this teaching to encourage someone else?

10. What else is the Holy Spirit teaching me about the ministry of Jesus?

Who can you invite to church? Pray for them by name.
Who can you invite to Bible study? Pray for them by name.
Who can you bring to Jesus? Pray for them by name.

Chapter 2

SALT OF THE EARTH
From the Sermon on the Mount (Matt. 5:13)

Salt Production, 1670

Salt is good,
but if the salt has lost its saltiness,
how will you make it salty again?
Have salt in yourselves, and
be at peace with one another.
(Mark 9:50)

Salted with Fire

Everyone will be salted with fire (holy power).
Mark 9:49

Fire can destroy or fire can purify. They might seem like opposites, but they are not when it comes to purification. God is like a refiner's fire who can purify us from all unrighteousness. When we let God purify us with his holy grace, He will remove ungodliness one step at a time. He might even prune a branch that consists of good fruit, so that we will be even more fruitful. When we walk with Him, He will season us with His power. Jesus taught us the following metaphor to show us His work in us is good.

"Everyone will be salted with fire" (Mark 9:49).

We will cover the following topics in this chapter:

- DAY 1 – Miracles - Confirm a Message from a Messenger
- DAY 2 – Beatitudes and Rewards
- DAY 3 – Get Right with God (everyday)
- DAY 4 - God Provides Salt (yesterday, today, and tomorrow)
- DAY 5 - Five Purposes of Salt
- DAY 6 - Put on the Full Armor of God

Sing: Refiner's Fire

Purify my heart, let me be as gold, and precious silver.
Purify my heart, let me be as gold, pure gold.
Refiner's fire, my heart's one desire, is to be holy.
Set apart for you, Lord, I choose to be holy.
Set apart for you, My Master, ready to do Your will.

DAY 1 - Miracles

In what way was Jesus seasoned with salt (holy power)? He had authority to forgive, wisdom to speak messages, a desire to teach us about the kingdom of God on earth, and the ability to do miracles. Jesus performed several miracles before he gave his famous Sermon on the Mount. He spoke to a group of people who were willing to listen and learn. Up to this point, Jesus had been baptized by John the Baptist and was tested in the wilderness. He had been teaching in Synagogues and preaching from the written Word of God. He announced, "Repent, for the kingdom of heaven has come." Jesus chose his twelve disciples prior to the Sermon on the Mount. He performed miracles to confirm that he is the Son of God - sent by God – with a powerful message of hope and grace. People responded in various ways to the miracles of Jesus. Below, let us examine various ways people were responding to these miracles.

1. **Water into Wine** – Read John 2:11 below.
   Did the disciples of Jesus *believe in Jesus* at the time when Jesus turned water into wine?

   This, the first of his signs, Jesus did at Cana in Galilee, and manifested his glory. And his disciples believed in him.
   (John 2:11)

   Manifest his glory means to show a divine nature, make it apparent.

2. **Healing an Official Son's Illness** –
   Read John 4:53 below.
   After Jesus healed the official's son from an illness, the father believed in Jesus. Who else believed in Jesus?

   The father knew that was the hour when Jesus had said to him, "Your son will live." And he himself believed, and all his household.
   (John 4:53)

3. **Man Delivered from an Unclean Spirit** –
   Read Luke 4:36 below.
   What did the people say about Jesus delivering people from an unclean spirit?

   > *And they were all amazed and said to one another, "What is this word? For with authority and power he commands the unclean spirits, and they come out!"*
   > (Luke 4:36)

4. **Speak the GOOD NEWS** – Read Luke 4:42.
   Why did Jesus move on to another town?

   > *…but Jesus said to them, "I must preach the good news of the kingdom of God to the other towns as well; for I was sent for this purpose."*
   > (Luke 4:42)

   Pray for five of your neighbors to hear the good news Gospel message.
   Write their first name below and pray for their salvation.
   If they are already saved, pray for their sanctification.

28

5. **Catching a Large Number of Fish** – Simon Peter had been fishing all night and caught nothing. He thought he knew more about fishing than Jesus. Just when all seemed hopeless, Jesus said, "Let down the nets for a catch." At first, Peter was doubtful he would catch anything. Then Peter decided to do what Jesus told him to do. Much to his surprise, the catch was more than he ever imagined.

   Read Luke 5:8 below.

   How did Simon Peter respond to Jesus after they caught an incredibly large number of fish?

   But when Simon Peter saw it, he fell down at Jesus' knees, saying, "Depart from me, for I am a sinful man, O Lord."
   (Luke 5:8)

6. **A Leper Cleansed** – After Jesus healed a leper, the man went out and spread the news even though Jesus instructed him to "say nothing to anyone...but go show yourself to the priest and offer for your cleansing what Moses commanded, for a proof to them."

   What was the consequence of the man's disobedience?
   Read Mark 1:45 below.

   But the cleansed leper went out and began to talk freely about it, and to spread the news, so that Jesus could no longer openly enter a town, but was out in desolate places, and people were coming to him from every quarter.
   (Mark 1:45)

   Dear Lord, we want the healing. We want You, the Healer.
   Help us obey your Word. Amen.

7. **Healing a Paralytic (Paralyzed man)** - Jesus has authority to forgive us of all our sins. He said, "The Son of Man has authority on earth to forgive sins." One day, some people lowered a paralyzed man through a roof to get to Jesus. When Jesus saw what the man's friends were doing, Jesus recognized the friend's faith in action. He knew the paralyzed man needed both healing and forgiveness. Jesus told the paralyzed man, "Friend, your sins are forgiven. Take up your mat and go home." There will be times when we need to make a great effort to bring our paralyzed friends to Jesus.

Read Luke 5:26 below.

And amazement seized them all, and they glorified God and were filled with awe, saying, "We have seen extraordinary things today." (Luke 5:26)

How did the people respond to Jesus's incredible power to heal? Check all that apply.

- o They were amazed.
- o They glorified God.
   They were filled with awe.
- o They admitted out loud they saw extraordinary things that day.

Personal question: How have you responded to the miracles of Jesus?

A. Feeling unworthy like Peter – Fall on my knees before Jesus.

B. Filled with amazement - Wow! Praise God! I believe even though I have not seen it myself! Thank you, God, for sending us Jesus your one and only, amazing Son! I love the divine nature of Jesus!!

C. An investigator like Lee Strobel or J Warner Wallace - I wonder if Jesus really healed people and performed miracles. Maybe he did, but maybe he didn't. I need to look into it more.

D. Reject it like a Pharisee - Even if I saw Jesus do a miracle, I would not believe it.

8. **Restoring a Withered Hand** – Jesus is very familiar with the connection between the human mind and emotions. After Jesus had been teaching in synagogues and healing people, the scribes and Pharisees were filled with fury. One Sabbath day, Jesus knew the scribes and Pharisees were angry that he was forgiving sins and healing people. Note: Today, it is clinically proven that anger is always caused by angry thoughts. So, Jesus redirected their angry thoughts by asking a question. "Is it lawful on the Sabbath to do good or do harm, to save life or destroy it?" Jesus performed a miracle of restoring a withered hand on the Sabbath. Why were the scribes and Pharisees angry that Jesus healed on the Sabbath? They needed to learn it is good to heal and save life even on the Sabbath.

Read how the Pharisees responded in Luke 6:11 below.

But they were filled with fury and discussed with one another what they might do to Jesus.

What did James, the brother of Jesus, say to do about anger?

Read James 1:19-21 below.

Know this, my beloved brothers: let every person be quick to hear, slow to speak, slow to anger; for the anger of man does not produce the righteousness of God. Therefore put away all filthiness and rampant wickedness and receive with meekness the implanted word, which is able to save your souls.

9. **No Miracle** –

Why does Jesus sometimes not perform a miracle?

And he did not do many mighty works there, because of their unbelief. (Matthew 13:58)

DAY 2 – Beatitudes

Jesus began the Sermon on the Mount by teaching "Beatitudes." It is important to understand each one of these beatitudes (i. e. good attitudes). Below, you will find eight beatitudes and a short explanation of what they mean. Then we will learn a corresponding reward (i. e. a blessing) for each one from Matthew 5:2-11.

- Poor in spirit – Know we need God's help.
- Mourn – Express godly sorry over a loss.
- Meek – Remain humble, strong, and gentle.
- Hunger and thirst for righteousness – Desire for divinity and holiness.
- Merciful – Extend compassion to others.
- Pure in heart – Desire what is good and right in God's sight.
- Peacemakers – Make a calm effort to reconcile.
- Persecuted for righteousness' sake – Do what is good and right in God's sight even when others oppose.

Verse 2: And he opened his mouth and taught them, saying:

Verse 3: *"Blessed are the poor in spirit, for theirs is the kingdom of heaven.*

Verse 4: *"Blessed are those who mourn, for they shall be comforted.*

Verse 5: *"Blessed are the meek, for they shall inherit the earth.*

Verse 6: *"Blessed are those who hunger and thirst for righteousness, for they shall be satisfied.*

Verse 7: *"Blessed are the merciful, for they shall receive mercy.*

Verse 8: *"Blessed are the pure in heart, for they shall see God.*

Verse 9: "Blessed are the peacemakers, for they shall be called sons-of God.

Verse 10: *"Blessed are those who are persecuted for righteousness' sake, for theirs is the kingdom of heaven.*

Verse 11: *"Blessed are you when others revile you and persecute you and utter all kinds of evil against you falsely on my account. Rejoice and be glad, for your reward is great in heaven, for so they persecuted the prophets who were before you."*

Thank you, Lord, for these divine promises. Amen.

1. Read eight beatitudes below and give thanks to the Lord for each corresponding divine promise. Blessings are given to those who mourn, experience desperation, remain humble, seek divinity, give mercy, remain pure-hearted, make peace, and stand for righteousness in the face of people who oppose goodness.

    Blessed are the poor in spirit. The Lord is near to people who are brokenhearted. He saves the contrite spirit. *Contrite* means feeling or expressing remorse or penitence. The Lord is close to the one who is crushed in spirit. He looks on favor to those who are contrite in spirit (See Psalm 34:18, 51:17; Isaiah 57:15, 66:2). A person who is "poor in spirit" means the person knows our human condition falls short of perfection. We know we need God's grace, love, comfort, teaching, and transforming help, moment by moment.

    What does God provide the person who knows we all need God?
    Read Matt. 5:3 below. Write down the divine promise.
      Blessed are the poor in spirit, for theirs is the kingdom of heaven.

2. **Blessed are those who mourn.** "Those who mourn" are sorry with godly sorrow over sin. For example, we experience godly sorrow for sinning when the Holy Spirit convicts us. We tell God we are sorry when we have sinned. As another example, we can tell others we are sorry when they lose a loved one. It is important to mourn in a healthy way after losing a loved one.

    What does God provide the person who expresses godly sorrow over a loss?
    Read Matthew 5:4 below. Write down the divine promise.
      Blessed are those who mourn, for they shall be comforted.

3. **Blessed are the meek.** Meek does not mean weak. *Meek* means a gentle spirit. A meek person can find strength in being humble, gentle, patient, and being still. Meek people know how to gain strength at certain times in silence.

   What does God provide the person who is humble, gentle, and patient? Read Matthew 5:5 below. Write down the divine promise.
   Blessed are the meek, for they shall inherit the earth.

4. **Blessed are those who hunger and thirst for righteousness.** These are people who want the way of righteousness in their own life. They seek having a divine touch from heaven.

   What does God provide the person who hungers and thirsts for divinity? Read Matthew 5:6 below. Write down the divine promise.
   Blessed are those who hunger and thirst for righteousness, for they shall be satisfied.

5. **Blessed are the merciful.** These people are forgiving toward other people. They are compassionate toward other people. When they see someone struggling, they care about what the person is going through. They help however they can.

   What does God provide the person who shows mercy? Read Matthew 5:7 below. Write down the divine promise.
   Blessed are the merciful, for they shall receive mercy.

6. **Blessed are the pure in heart.** These people are genuine before God; they stand with a clean conscience. They do not have idols. They let the Word of God cleanse their hearts and transform their minds. They truly desire what is good and right in God's sight.

   What does God provide those who stand with a clean conscience?
   Read Matthew 5:8 below. Write down the divine promise.
   Blessed are the pure in heart, for they shall see God.

7. **Blessed are the peacemakers.** These people are good at restoring relationships. They use wisdom, initiate reconciliation, remain calm, and truly care. They can identify a practical problem, work out differences, and find a good solution that works for everyone. They are not selfish or self-seeking.

   What does God provide the person who is a peacemaker?
   Read Matthew 5:9 below.
   Blessed are the peacemakers, for they shall be called sons (and daughters) of God.

8. **Blessed are those who are persecuted for righteousness sake.** These people desire what is good, but they also do what is good even when others oppose it.

   What does God provide the person who does what is right and good in God's sight even though others might oppose it?
   Read Matthew 5:10 below.
   Blessed are those who are persecuted for righteousness' sake, for theirs is the kingdom of heaven.

DAY 3 – Get Right with God

We are all called to get right with God. Jesus wants each one of us to be the salt of the earth (a.k.a. a salty saint). Today, the salt of the earth are believers who set a good example to love others the way Jesus Christ loves others. We improve culture and preserve society by standing up for truth, justice, and mercy in God's sight. We make the world a better place by helping others call on the name of the Father, Son, and Holy Spirit. We help save the world from moral decay.

How did Paul describe salty saints in Corinth?

Read 1 Cor. 1:2-3 below. Check all that apply.

To the church of God that is in Corinth, to those sanctified in Christ Jesus, called to be saints together with all those who in every place call upon the name of our Lord Jesus Christ, both their Lord and ours: Grace to you and peace from God our Father and the Lord Jesus Christ. (1 Cor. 1:2-3)

- o   Salty saints are the church of God
- o   Those sanctified in Christ Jesus
- o   Those called to be saints
- o   Those who call on the name of our Lord Jesus Christ
- o   Those who receive grace from God our Father and the Lord Jesus
- o   Those who receive peace from God our Father and the Lord Jesus

The salt of the earth is a parable. A parable tells us an earthly story with a valuable meaning. In the *salt of the earth* parable, the salty people on earth can be described as saints, the visible community of believers, followers of Jesus Christ, or the universal church. Paul refers to born again believers in various churches as *saints* in books such as Colossians, Ephesians, Philippians, 1 Corinthians, and Jude. Jesus teaches us a short parable, *Salt of the Earth* in the Sermon on the Mount, to emphasize our value on earth. If you are a born-again believer, you are a valuable saint on earth. One of our purposes in life is to be the salt of the earth. We are all called to be a vessel of truth, flowing with divine power, and showering God's love to those around us.

Today, we know the value of salt. Salt preserves, heals, and gives flavor. For example, we put salt on protein and vegetables to taste better. If we get a sore throat, we can gargle with salt water to reduce bacteria. Gargling with salt water is known to pull fluids from the throat tissue, which helps wash the virus out. Drinking salty, warm broth also comforts and heals. Salt continues to have the great value of preserving, healing, and giving flavor.

In the Old Testament, salt had the same great value of preserving, healing, and giving flavor. Salt was also added to animal sacrifice offerings for a person or group of people to get right with God. The offering had a pleasing aroma to the Lord. In the New Testament, Jesus Christ is the perfect Lamb of God who was without sin, our sin offering, who paid the penalty for all our sin, takes our sin away, and gives us power over sin (See Hebrews 2:17, 13:12).

1. **Sin Offering** - What did the Old Testament priests put salt on?

> Read Leviticus 2:13.
> *You shall season all your grain offerings with salt. You shall not let the salt of the covenant with your God be missing from your grain offering; with all your offerings you shall offer salt.*
> (Leviticus 2:13)

The five main types of offerings were as follows:
- Burnt Offering (Leviticus 1) most common
- Grain Offering (Leviticus 2)
- Peace Offering (Leviticus 3)
- Sin Offering (Leviticus 4)
- Guilt Offering (Leviticus 5)

People were allowed to eat some of the offerings but not all of them. For anyone concerned about sodium in salt, just remember that water dilutes sodium. Physical activity and potassium can also help balance sodium. Multiple types of drinking water include tap water, electrolyte water, purified water, distilled water, alkaline water, spring water, and mineral water.

2. **Covenant of Salt** - What is the *Covenant of Salt* in the Old Testament that King Abijah of Judah proclaimed to King Jeroboam and all of Israel? (See 2 Chronicles 13:1-12)

   Hint: Read verse 5.
   Ought you not to know that the LORD God of Israel gave the kingship over Israel forever to David and his sons by a covenant of salt?
   (2 Chronicles 13:5)

 "God ratified his covenant with David by salt."
-    Dr. Harold L. Willmington, Author of *Guide to the Bible*

   Ratify is a verb that means to make a contract, agreement, or treaty.

3. **Davidic Covenant** - The Covenant of Salt is also called the *Davidic Covenant*. The line of David will always have the right to rule over Israel.

   What is the Davidic Covenant that Nathan the prophet prophesied to King David?

   (See 1 Chronicles 17:11-15)

   Read 1 Chronicles 17:14 below.

   > *...but I will confirm him in my house and in my kingdom forever, and his throne shall be established forever.*

4. **Eternal Kingdom** - The New Testament refers to King David over fifty times. In the verses below, find out in what way Jesus Christ fulfilled the Davidic Covenant (i.e. Covenant of Salt).

   What did the angel Gabriel promise to Mary?

   Read Luke 1:32-33 below.

   > *He will be great and will be called the Son of the Most High. And the Lord God will give to him the throne of his father David, and he will reign over the house of Jacob forever, and of his kingdom there will be no end.*

5. **Faithful to Keep Promises** - The Covenant of Salt was declared and prophesied by many prophets such as Abraham, Moses, and Nathan. God blesses prophets who know the divine promises of God and declare them. From the days of Nathan the prophet to the days of the angel, Gabriel, who spoke to Mary, God kept his promise to establish His divine kingdom forever.

    How many generations are listed from the following:

    - Abraham to King David
    - King David the Babylonian captivity
    - Babylonian captivity to the Lord Jesus Christ

    Read Matthew 1:17 below.

    So all the generations from Abraham to David were fourteen generations, and from David to the deportation to Babylon fourteen generations, and from the deportation to Babylon to the Christ fourteen generations.

6. **Jesus! Have Mercy on Me!** - God promised to establish his eternal kingdom, and his eternal kingdom has been established. The throne of King David was given to the Lord Jesus Christ. During the 3-year ministry of Jesus, we see a record of Jesus helping people who call on his name especially those who have faith. A blind beggar named Bartimaeus called out to Jesus in faith. "Jesus, Son of David, have mercy on me!" Many rebuked the blind beggar and told him to be quiet. Again, he cried out, "Son of David, have mercy on me!"

Even though some people were telling Bartimaeus to be quiet, the blind beggar continued to call out to Jesus for healing.

Who does God give salvation to?

> ...for, *"Everyone who calls on the name of the Lord will be saved."* (Romans 10:13, Acts 2:21)

> *And everyone who calls on the name of the LORD will be saved; for on Mount Zion and in Jerusalem there will be deliverance, as the LORD has promised, among the remnant called by the LORD.* (Joel 2:32)

Personal question – Do you know for sure you will go to heaven after your physical body dies?

7. **Pay Close Attention** - What is a *salty* saint? A salty saint is a believer who stands up for what is good and right in God's sight. A salty saint is a child of God who loves others so much that other people feel thirsty for the Living Water. We need salty saints to help stop corruption and wicked behavior. Jesus refers to his church of believers as the salt of the earth.

What do you find important or comforting in King Solomon's prayer found in 2 Chronicles 6:14-17?

"O LORD, God of Israel, there is no God like you, in heaven or on earth, keeping covenant and showing steadfast love to your servants who walk before you with all their heart, who have kept with your servant David my father what you declared to him. You spoke with your mouth, and with your hand have fulfilled it this day. Now therefore, O LORD, God of Israel, keep for your servant David my father what you have promised him, saying,

'You shall not lack a man to sit before me on the throne of Israel, if only your sons pay close attention to their way, to walk in my law as you have walked before me.'

Now therefore, O LORD, God of Israel, let your word be confirmed, which you have spoken to your servant David."

Dear Lord,

Help me pay attention to what I am saying and doing. Help me pay attention to my thoughts and behavior. Help me know how to take my thoughts captive to the obedience of Christ. I want to put off the ungodly way and put on the godly way. I want to be the salt of the earth and salted with your divine power. I honor your name. Help me stand up for what is good and right in Your sight. Thank you for the grace you have given to us in Jesus Christ as our Lord and Savior. I love You. Help me love others the way you want me to. Amen

DAY 4 - God Provides a Mineral Called Salt

Salt is important. Salt therapy rooms are available in some places today as an alternative treatment for lung problems such as asthma, bronchitis, or a cough. Salt therapy is called halotherapy. The therapy room provides tiny salt particles to help improve your breathing. Another salt treatment regimen involves using an over-the-counter saline nose spray on a regular basis or as needed during pollen season. Salt is a valuable mineral on earth. It always has been a valuable substance. Salt is a mineral made primarily of sodium and chloride ($NaCl$), bonded together to help as an electrolyte, which help nerves and muscles to function correctly.

1. **Required in the Temple** - What important items did the priests in Jerusalem require for the Lord's temple? Read Ezra 6:9 below.

   And whatever is needed—bulls, rams, or sheep for burnt offerings to the God of heaven, wheat, salt, wine, or oil, as the priests at Jerusalem require—let that be given to them day by day without fail…

   List at least seven items from Ezra 6:9 below that are mentioned.

2. **Salty Wisdom** - In the salt parable, Jesus knows we are supposed to be the salt of the earth. He instructed us to not lose our saltiness. The natural question is to ask how a person can be the salt of the earth and not lose the flavor of being salty.

If a believer wants to be the salt of the earth, what is required for the beginning of wisdom?

Read Proverbs 9:10. What is required for wisdom?

The <u>fear of the LORD</u> is the beginning of wisdom, and the <u>knowledge of the Holy One</u> is insight.

1.

2.

Read Psalm 111:10. What do we get for practicing wisdom?

The fear of the LORD is the beginning of wisdom; all those who practice it have a <u>good understanding</u>. His praise endures forever!

Read Proverbs 4:7 below.

The beginning of wisdom is this: Get wisdom, and whatever you get, get insight.

Read Job 28:28 below. In addition to having a healthy fear of the Lord (i.e respecting the Lord with great awe and reverence) and knowledge of the Holy One, how else do we gain wisdom?

And he said to man, 'Behold, the fear of the Lord, that is wisdom, and to <u>turn away from evil</u> is understanding.'"

3.

In addition to having a healthy fear of the Lord, gaining knowledge of the Holy One, and turning away from evil, what else can we do to gain wisdom?

Read Psalm 119:103-105 below.

How sweet are <u>your words</u> to my taste, sweeter than honey to my mouth! Through <u>your precepts</u> I get understanding; therefore, I hate every false way.

Your word is a lamp to my feet and a light to my path.

4.

5.

Recap - Five ways to be a salty saint include having the fear of the Lord, knowledge of the Holy One, turn away from evil, receive God's Word like honey, and receive God's precepts. Precepts are biblical principles.

3. **Salty Works** - James, the half-brother of Jesus, explained the importance of <u>taming the tongue</u>.

   Read James 3:14-16 below. Underline several ungodly behaviors and consequences of unwashed hearts.

   But if you have bitter jealousy and selfish ambition in your hearts, do not boast and be false to the truth. This is not the wisdom that comes down from above, but is earthly, unspiritual, demonic. For where jealousy and selfish ambition exist, there will be disorder and every vile practice.

   Read James 3:13, 17-18 below. Now underline several godly behaviors and good results.

   Who is wise and understanding among you? By his good conduct let him show his works in the meekness of wisdom…But the wisdom from above is first pure, then peaceable, gentle, open to reason, full of mercy and good fruits, impartial and sincere. And a harvest of righteousness is sown in peace by those who make peace.

   When we are faced with a disagreement, dispute, or conflict, we need to pray for wisdom and extend an olive branch of peace and hope. It is important to first desire what is good, then express reason, mercy, good fruit – all impartial and sincere. It is healthy to desire a peaceful resolution while remaining steadfast to end a difficult situation.

4. **Salty Speech** - We are instructed to let our speech always be with grace and seasoned with salt. What is the purpose of having salty speech?

   Read Colossians 4:6 below.

   Let your speech always be <u>gracious</u>, seasoned with salt, so that you may know how you ought to answer each person.

5. **Salty Life** - Salt causes one to be thirsty, which is a symbol for a salty saint causing an unbeliever to produce a thirst for God. Salt and fire represent the inward work of the Holy Spirit and the Word of God in a person's life, transforming people to be more holy. We are transformed by the renewing of our mind when the Holy Spirit overrides His will in our life and purifies us like pure gold. Then we are able to bear good fruit, speak how He wants us to speak, and do the good work He has called us to do.

   Mark plainly tells us where we need to have salt. Where do we need salt?

   Read Mark 9:50 below.

   Salt is good, but if the salt has lost its saltiness, how will you make it salty again? Have salt in yourselves, and <u>be at peace with one another</u>.

   Recap: Salty saints will have the fear of the Lord, knowledge of the Holy One, turn away from doing evil, love the Word of God, live out biblical principles, tame the tongue, and be at peace with one another.

6. **Salty Flavor** -JUST FOR FUN!
   What kind of food might Job prefer to put salt on?

   Read Job 6:6 below.

   Can flavorless food be eaten without salt? Or is there any taste in the white of an egg?

   What kind of healthy, salty food do you like?

   - o   Salted nuts

   - o   Green olives

   - o   Black olives

   - o   Cheese and crackers

   - o   Salted cucumber slices

   - o   Eggs: Deviled eggs, scrambled, etc.

   - o   Carrots and dip or hummus

   - o   Soup, cooked vegetables

   - o   Ants on a Log

   - o   Other: _____

TO DO: Make a charcuterie board with healthy, salty foods.

DAY 5 – **Salt of the Earth**

Simply put, your salty life matters. God made you in his image and He loves you with everlasting love. This means your life has meaning and purpose. He wants you to be the *salt of the earth*. He wants to purify you in a personal relationship with the Father, Son, and Holy Spirit. He wants you to trust Jesus as your personal Savior, give you wisdom, bless your speech, and help you do good work.

Jesus used the parable "salt of the earth" to describe how God wants us to be good, honest, humble people. He helps us live out the important task of making a great contribution to society, preserve society, and help save the world from moral decay. He wants us to speak truth, do good work, love justice and mercy, and walk humbly in step with the Holy Spirit. As a salty saint, we can bring hope and peace to others who are hurting, lost, and brokenhearted.

1. **Warning** - What is the warning if we are not salty?

   Read Matthew 5:13 below.

   You are the salt of the earth; but if the salt loses its flavor, how shall it be seasoned? It is then good for nothing but to be <u>thrown out</u> and <u>trampled underfoot</u> by men.

Jesus says we are to function as the *salt of the earth*.
Here are five main purposes of salt:

- Flavor – Have you noticed divine promises that God provides for us in life? If not, go back to the rewards listed in the Beatitudes.

- Preserve – Have you made a decision to prevent or stop corruption in your community? Edmund Bruke once said, "The only thing necessary for the triumph of evil is for good men to do nothing." Erin Gruwell once said, "Evil prevails when good people do nothing."

- Sacrificing – Do you offer up your life daily to God? Praise God even when it's tough. Seek His will all the time. Welcome Him in every area of your life.

- Judgement – Do you judge evil behavior? It's easy to not get involved, but we are called to judge with right judgement (More on this in Chapter 3).

- Fertilizing – Are you doing kingdom work? We use the right amount of fertilizers on the ground so that plowing is easier, plants are nourished, weeds are killed, crops are protected from disease, and the results increase.

  Disciples are the salt of the earth because our job is to enrich every area, stimulate growth, plant, water, and let life grow up in new places.

2. **Five Purposes** - Do you think Jesus wants you to be available for all five purposes? Explain.

3. **Five Ways to be Salty** – Life is much better when the Holy Spirit is flowing through your life. Jesus calls us to be the salt of the earth.

   How can you be the *salt of the earth*? Using the verses below, practice explaining to someone how they can be the salt of the earth.

   Read Acts 16:31.
   So they said, "Believe on the Lord Jesus Christ, and you will be saved, you and your household."

   Read Colossians 4:6.
   Let your speech always be with grace, seasoned with salt, that you may know how you ought to answer each one.

   Read Mark 9:50.
   Salt is good, but if the salt has lost its saltiness, how will you make it salty again? Have salt in yourselves, and be at peace with one another.

Read Romans 12:1-2.
I beseech you therefore, brethren, by the mercies of God, that you present your bodies a living sacrifice, holy, acceptable to God, which is your reasonable service. And do not be conformed to this world, but be transformed by the renewing of your mind, that you may prove what is that good and acceptable and perfect will of God.

Read Matthew 28:19-20.
Go therefore and make disciples of all nations, baptizing them in the name of the Father and of the Son and of the Holy Spirit, teaching them to observe all that I have commanded you. And behold, I am with you always, to the end of the age.

4. **Boast in the Lord** - We are not supposed to boast in wisdom, strength, nor riches (See Jeremiah 9:23). We are not to boast in the person who gave us a water baptism nor any pastor or priest we find today. Jesus Christ is the wisdom and power of God who provides salvation. We need to remember to share the gospel message of Jesus Christ. If we do boast, we are instructed to boast in the Lord.

How can salty saints boast in the Lord? Using the verses below, practice explaining to someone how the LORD is more wonderful than anything.

Read 1 Corinthians 1:31 below.

And because of God, you are in Christ Jesus, who became to us wisdom from God, righteousness and sanctification and redemption, so that, as it is written, "Let the one who boasts, boast in the Lord."

Read Jeremiah 9:24 below.

...but let him who boasts boast in this, that he understands and knows me, that I am the LORD who practices steadfast love, justice, and righteousness in the earth. For in these things I delight, declares the LORD.

5. **Judge Behavior** - Believers are instructed to judge other people's behavior. When we judge appropriately, we are not condemning. When we judge, we truthfully observe behavior, and judge it according to God's standard of living.

   In what way are salty saints to judge others? Describe two main aspects of the right way to judge, according to John 7:24 below.

   Do not judge by appearances, but judge with right judgment.

6. **Nourish Your Soul** - At the end of a forty-day journey in the wilderness, Jesus was tempted three times by the devil. Feeling hungry, Jesus was tempted to turn a stone into bread. Jesus answered, "It is written, 'Man shall not live by bread alone." (Luke 4:4).

   Jesus was quoting a verse from Deuteronomy 8:3, which explains that mankind shall not live by bread alone. In addition to eating food for nourishment, what is mankind to live on?

   Read Deuteronomy 8:3 below.

   And he humbled you and let you hunger and fed you with manna, which you did not know, nor did your fathers know, that he might make you know that man does not live by bread alone, but man lives by every word that comes from the mouth of the LORD (Yahweh).

DAY 6 – Put on the whole Armor of God

PERSONAL APPLICATION - The sword of the Spirit is the Word of God. Please keep in mind, some people are comfortable sharing personal things, but others are not. We are to use the written Word of God, not misuse it (Ephesians 6:10-20).

1. In the teaching, Salt of the Earth from Matthew 5:13, is there a sin to avoid?

    Jesus warns us to not lose our salty flavor as a born-again believer.

    Read Hebrews 10:29 below. Write down three sins to avoid from the following verse.

    How much more severely do you think one deserves to be punished who has <u>trampled on the Son of God</u>, <u>profaned the blood of the covenant</u> that sanctified him, and <u>insulted the Spirit of grace</u>?

2. Is there a divine promise to trust? If so, what is it?

    As the Saltiest of all, Jesus kept the Father's commands and remained in the Father's love. When the *salt of the earth* obeys the words of Jesus, Jesus promises that we will bear good fruit.

    Read John 15:11 below. Identify the promise for keeping the Words of Jesus active in our life.

    These things I have spoken to you, that my joy may be in you, and that your joy may be full.

3. Is there a command to obey in the parable of the salt of the earth? If so, what is it?

    Read John 15:12 below.

    This is my commandment, that you love one another as I have loved you.
    (John 15:12)

4. What does this passage say about God's character, his nature, or his work?

   Read John 15:15-16 below.

   No longer do I call you servants, for the servant does not know what his master is doing; but I have called you friends, for all that I have heard from my Father I have made known to you. You did not choose me, but I chose you and appointed you that you should go and bear fruit and that your fruit should abide, so that whatever you ask the Father in my name, he may give it to you.

5. What does this passage say about mankind?

   Read John 15:17 below.

   These things I command you, so that you will love one another.

6. Is there an example to follow?

    Read John 15:12 below.

    This is my commandment, that you love one another as I have loved you.

7. How can John 16:27 be a personal prayer of thanksgiving? Fill your name in below.

    ...for the Father himself loves you, because you (saints) have loved me (Jesus) and have believed that I (Jesus) came from God.

    Thank you, Father God,

    for loving me _____,

    because I _____ love Jesus,

    and I believe that Jesus came from God.

8. What verse can I meditate on?
    (John 16:33)

    I have said these things to you, that in me you may have peace. In the world you will have tribulation. But take heart; I have overcome the world.

9. How can I develop biblical affirmations and encourage someone else?

    I am the salt of the earth.
    I have value and purpose.
    I make a positive impact in the culture.
    I bear good fruit.
    I make a real difference in the world.
    I like to share the gospel and give a reason for the hope of eternal life.
    I love one another how Jesus loved one another.

10. How else is the Holy Spirit teaching you?

    Who can you invite to church? Pray for them by name.
    Who can you invite to Bible study? Pray for them by name.
    Who can you bring to Jesus? Pray for them by name.

Notes:

Chapter 3

PARABLES OF JESUS
Let Your Light Shine
Spec and Log: How to Judge/Lead
Two Gates
House on a Rock
New Wine

Sermon on the Mount by Henrik Olrik (1830-1890)

DAY 1 – Parable of "Let Your Light Shine"

Jesus teaches us a parable of letting your light shine. About one-third of the teachings of Jesus in the Gospel books are in parabolic form. The purpose of giving us a parable is to use an earthly story we are familiar with to give us a spiritual truth. Parables are for sincere people to understand a lesson about the kingdom of heaven on earth. The story can very well make it difficult for insincere people to understand the lesson. A sincere heart can learn a spiritual truth, prophecy, and divine authority from a parable.

Jesus gave us five parables in the Sermon on the Mount. We already covered Salt of the Earth in the last chapter. We can find more than forty parables in the Gospel books, but in this chapter, we will go through five parables, four from the Sermon on the Mount and one other, New Wine, that Jesus taught later.

When we let our light shine, we are living the way we are meant to live. Our light can help other people find their way out of the dark, but our light shines only when the Light of the World is shining through us.

Read the *Let Your Light Shine* parable below from Matthew 5:14-16.

"You are the light of the world. A city set on a hill cannot be hidden. Nor do people light a lamp and put it under a basket, but on a stand, and it gives light to all in the house. In the same way, let your light shine before others, so that they may see your good works and give glory to your Father who is in heaven."

List what kind of good works your church or city is doing.

Session Three: Parables

How can we let our light shine? Check all that apply:

- ○ Cherish his Word in our life.
- ○ Coordinate Bible study groups.
- ○ Support gospel-centered ministries.
- ○ Use the gift of service in ministry.
- ○ Use the gift of declaring God's love and mercy.
- ○ Use your gifts in kingdom work.
- ○ Share my salvation testimony.
- ○ Live out a blameless life in peace and love.
- ○ Point others to Jesus.
- ○ Give light to everyone in my house.
- ○ Walk in truth.
- ○ Take a meal to someone.
- ○ Pray with someone.

How can we encourage people in other countries let their light shine?
Check all that apply:

- ○ Food banks, pack meals, serve meals
- ○ Hospitals, doctors, nurses, eye glasses, dental care
- ○ Care for homeless: food, clothes, blankets, toiletries, teach reading and math, organize field trips, get businesses to help, help them stick with a decent job, provide mental support.
- ○ Shelter, build houses, community facilities, parks, farms, playgrounds, athletic facilities
- ○ Clothes, laundry services, shoes, undergarments, jackets
- ○ Love God, praise God, get to know God's good work
- ○ Character building, inspiration for good morals
- ○ Farmer's market, provide healthy fruit and vegetables and soup
- ○ Support groups, prayer groups, addiction recovery groups
- ○ Traffic procedures, travel routes, bike trails, hiking trails
- ○ Local products, local market, trade goods
- ○ Support good leaders
- ○ Respect good police, respect good authority
- ○ Cleanliness, soap, good hygiene, brush teeth

1. **Show Good Work** - Let others see your good works and glorify God (See Matthew 5:16). First, it's important to know we are not saved by our good works (See Ephesians 2:8-10). Nevertheless, we are saved by grace for good works. What kind of good work can we do?

   Circle two things you can share with your family and neighbors.

   Read Luke 3:11 and 1 John 3:17.
   And he answered them, "Whoever has two tunics is to share with him who has none, and whoever has food is to do likewise."

   Circle three good works below.

   Read James 1:27.

   Religion that is pure and undefiled before God the Father is this: to visit orphans and widows in their affliction, and to keep oneself unstained from the world.

   Circle two ways to provide.

   Read 1 Timothy 5:8.

   But if anyone does not provide for his relatives, and especially for members of his household, he has denied the faith and is worse than an unbeliever.

64

2. **Share your salvation testimony**.
   Read Matthew 10:32-33 and Luke 8:39 below.

   *So, everyone who acknowledges me before men, I also will
   acknowledge before my Father who is in heaven, but whoever
   denies me before men, I also will deny before my Father who is in
   heaven.*

   *"Return to your home and declare how much God has done for
   you." And the man went away, proclaiming throughout the whole
   city how much Jesus had done for him.*

   When did you accept Jesus Christ as your personal Savior?

   Describe what the Gospel message means.
   (See 1 Corinthians 15:1-8)

   List at least one way your life is better with Jesus as your Lord and Savior.

3. **Walk in Truth** - We let our light shine when we walk in truth. Eve was deceived by a serpent who was not speaking truth. The reason the serpent spoke falsehoods is because Satan is a liar (See John 8:44). Satan tries to devour people, steal from people, destroy truth, and demolish God's Word (See 1 Peter 5:8).

   What does *truth* mean? Truth does not mean opinion or preferences. Truth corresponds to reality, to the way things really are. The Bible says God cannot lie (See Titus 1:2), so God only speaks truth. Jesus said he is Truth (See John 14:6). Jesus is Truth because Jesus is God in the flesh (See John 1:14). The Holy Spirit is also called the Spirit of Truth (See John 16:13). We find 100% truth in the Trinity: in the Father, Son, and Holy Spirit.

   In his high priestly prayer, what does Jesus pray for?

   Read John 17:17 below.

   Sanctify them in the truth; your word is truth.

   "The definition of truth is the agreement of thoughts with reality."
   - Mortimer J. Adler, American Philosopher,
       Author of *Truth in Religion*

4. **Truth Sets Us Free** - What does the truth do in a person's life?

Read John 8:31-32 below.

So Jesus said to the Jews who had believed him, "If you abide in my word, you are truly my disciples, and you will know the truth, and the truth will set you free."

Truth is vitally important. One of the Ten Commandments is "Thou shall not lie."

Read Leviticus 19:11 below.
Do not steal. Do not lie. Do not deceive one another.

In psychology, there are Grounding Techniques to help reduce anxiety and improve your mood. The theory believes that if we use our five senses accurately, then we can help calm our worries. Some people use the "5-4-3-2-1" technique that goes like this: Name 5 things you see, 4 things you feel, 3 things you hear, 2 things you smell, and 1 thing you taste. When you force your thoughts on truth by using your senses, the truth is "setting you free" from falsehood as Jesus explains in John 8:32.

Pray for five of your neighbors to hear the good news Gospel message.
Write their first name below and pray for their salvation.
If they are already saved, pray for their sanctification.

5. **Live a Blameless Life** - List seven ways God described Job. Read Job 2:3 below.

> *Then the LORD said to Satan, "Have you considered My servant Job? For there is no one on earth like him, a man who is blameless and upright, who fears God and shuns evil. He still retains his integrity, even though you incited Me against him to ruin him without cause."*

- _____

- _____

- _____

- _____

- _____

- _____

- _____

Dear Lord God Almighty, I want to be blameless and upright. I respect You for who You are, the greatest of all and mighty all the time. Help me and my family to shun evil and retain our integrity. Amen.

"To those involved in this dying world, Satan will come with evil's undiluted power to deceive, for they have refused the truth which could have saved them... They see truth as a lie, and the lie as the truth. They accept the lies of the devil."
- Billy Graham, American Evangelist

6. **Hold Fast to the Word of Life** -
Read Philippians 2:14-16 below. Circle all the things that describe a blameless person and underline all the things a blameless person does not do.

Do all things without grumbling or disputing, that you may be blameless and innocent, children of God without blemish in the midst of a crooked and twisted generation, among whom you shine as lights in the world, holding fast to the word of life, so that in the day of Christ I may be proud that I did not run in vain or labor in vain.

Lord, help me and my family shine as a light in the world. Amen.

7. **Redeemed People** - 144,000 blameless people who are redeemed stand on Mount Zion with the Lamb, singing a new song.

What do blameless people NOT do?

Read Revelation 14:5 below.

...and in their mouth no lie was found, for they are blameless.

8. **City on a Hill** - Jesus is the Light of the world, and we are the light of the world. Notice the capitol L and the lowercase l. The only way you can be the light of the world is when the Light of the world is shining through you. Salty saints are not hidden. We let the Light of God shine through us.

Read Matthew 5:14 below.
You are the light of the world. A city set on a hill cannot be hidden.

Paul let his light shine when he confronted Elymus the magician. At least two more people were there, a Jewish false prophet named Bar-Jesus and a man of intelligence named Sergius Paulus, a proconsul. Filled with the Holy Spirit and power, Paul gave the magician a rebuke. *"You son of the devil, you enemy of all righteousness, full of all deceit and villainy, will you not stop making crooked the straight paths of the Lord? And now, behold, the hand of the Lord is upon you, and you will be blind and unable to see the sun for a time." (Acts 13:10-11)*

Apostle Paul   Elymus   Bar-Jesus   Sergius Paulus

What did proconsul Sergius Paulus do when he saw the light shining in Paul?

Read Acts 13:12 below.

Then the proconsul believed, when he saw what had occurred, for he was astonished at the teaching of the Lord.

9. **Divine Light** - Luke pointed out that no one lights a lamp and puts it under a bed. Rather, we light a lamp and let those who enter the house see the light. He affirmed that everything will be made known and brought to light.

   What does Luke tell us to be careful about doing?

   Read Luke 8:18 below.

   Take care then how you hear, for to the one who has, more will be given, and from the one who has not, even what he thinks that he has will be taken away.

   We can experience abundant life when we let divine Light shine through us. We let Salt work in our life. We do that by welcoming divine transformation in a personal relationship with the Father, Son, and Holy Spirit. We are like a kernel of wheat that falls to the ground and dies, but it grows and produces much more than a single seed that remains in darkness. Salty saints are not stuffed under the bed. We are not hidden. Instead of being a seed that exists in loneliness, Jesus gives us the kernel of wheat analogy to show us it is fruitful to live in fellowship with the Father, Son, and Holy Spirit.
   (See John 12:24-26)

DAY 2 – Parable of the Spec and Log (How to Judge)

Jesus spoke in parables to teach us lessons and give us guidance, which fulfills Old Testament prophecy. We find a prophetic word in Psalm 78:2.

"I will open my mouth in parables; I will utter things hidden from the beginning."

The Bible uses many types of figures of speech, perhaps over two hundred types of figures of speech in over five thousand passages. For example, hyperbole, metaphor, paradox, and a simile, are all figures of speech. A *parable* often uses a familiar situation to teach us a more important lesson. When a word, term, or saying is difficult to understand at first glance, sometimes we call it a *mystery*. For example, many people have a difficult time with the word *trinity*. We say that God is three in one, but how is that so? We can understand a little bit better by using a triangle to show three corners on one triangle. A difficult saying can also be called *enigmatic*, which means difficult to interpret. For example, what does "changed in the twinkling of an eye" mean? To many believers, it means *rapture*, a time when God changes a believer from mortality to immortality. The study of interpretation is called hermeneutics. For example, the word *day* can mean during sunlight hours, a twenty-four-hour period, or a season of many years.

Trinity

Rapture

Day

At first glance, a saying might even seem to be a contradiction, but upon further study, we find the meaning to be true, which is called a *paradox*. For example, *"whoever tries to keep their life will lose it, but whoever loses their life will keep it"* (Luke 17:33) is another way of saying do not worship yourself. Rather, worship God. It might sound like a contradiction at first, but the meaning behind it is not a contradiction.

Read the Speck and Log parable from Matthew 7:1-5 below.

"Judge not, that you be not judged. For with the judgment you pronounce you will be judged, and with the measure you use it will be measured to you. Why do you see the speck that is in your brother's eye, but do not notice the log that is in your own eye? Or how can you say to your brother, 'Let me take the speck out of your eye,' when there is the log in your own eye? You hypocrite, first take the log out of your own eye, and then you will see clearly to take the speck out of your brother's eye."

Jesus further explained how to judge in John 7:24.

Do not judge by appearances, but judge with right judgment.

Find qualities of judges in Exodus 18:21.

Check all that apply.

- o   Men who fear God
- o   Trustworthy
- o   Hate a bribe

1. **Logs in the Eye** - When we judge a person's behavior, we always judge it according to some set of standard, either our own standard, God's standard, or someone else's standard. It is also important to distinguish between a human standard and a personal preference. God has given us his standard of holy living in the written Word of God, the Bible. His standard of good living also includes a moral law He put in our conscience (See Hebrews 8:11, Romans 2:15). When we judge what is right and wrong, we judge it according to a certain standard. God's standard is always based on truth. One of the problems we see in mankind is when people want to follow their own standard instead of following God's standard for good living.

   Review the following "logs" in the eye:

   - "There is no truth." Then is that true? No.

   - "Don't judge." Then is that judging? Yes.

   - "Stop shaming me." Then is that shaming? Possibly, depending if it's the Holy Spirit convicting sin or if it is slander, mocking, and insults.

   Discuss the logs mentioned above. Whose standard do you follow?

   A "log" is any kind of flaw in a person's behavior. An extremely controlling person might want to correct every flaw in someone's life as well as demand the person act and talk however the controlling person wants them to, that is, to their own standard.

   God's Word tells us that love does not demand one's own way.

   Read 1 Corinthians 13:4-6 below.

   > *Love is patient and kind; love does not envy or boast; it is not arrogant or rude. It does not insist on its own way; it is not irritable or resentful; it does not rejoice at wrongdoing, but rejoices with the truth.*

2. **Learn Divine Secrets** - In the written Word of God, we find helpful instructions for living a good life. These guidelines often are found in the following types of creative language:

   a.) Figures of speech to understand truth, beauty, and freedom
   b.) Stories and parables to illustrate a moral, lesson, precept, or principle

   In the parable of the Spec and Log, Jesus gives us insight into how to judge others properly. The Spec and Log parable is one of the most important parables for counselors, attorneys, judges, and any person who wants to be a leader, including leaders in education, church, family relationships, the community work, prison, hospitals, and politics. If you don't judge, you won't be a leader.

   What is the purpose of Jesus speaking in parables?
   Check all that apply. (See Matthew 13:10-17.)

   o   To know the secrets of the divine kingdom on earth
   o   To receive abundant life
   o   To understand more fully
   o   To receive inner healing
   o   To hear divine words for living a better life

   Read Matthew 13:11-13 below.

   > And Jesus answered them, "To you it has been given to know the secrets of the kingdom of heaven, but to them it has not been given.
   >
   > For to the one who has, more will be given, and he will have an abundance, but from the one who has not, even what he has will be taken away.
   >
   > This is why I speak to them in parables, because seeing they do not see, and hearing they do not hear, nor do they understand.

3. **Judge Rebellious Behavior** - First, we will judge rebellious behavior in the paragraph below from Psalm 78, *according to God's standard*. Then we will determine the better, godly way, *according to God's standard*.

   (See Psalm 78:8-11, 17-19, 20b-22, 31-33, 36-37, 40-42, 56-57).

   Ungodly behavior (sin) includes being stubborn in sin, rebelling against God, not faithful to God, not keeping God's covenant, not obeying God's laws, forgetting God's work, speaking well of God but not loving God in their heart, not remembering God saved them from their enemies, worshipping idols, and engaging in pagan worship at high places of immorality.

   What did the Israelites need to do? Check all that apply.

   - o   Turn away from sin each day.
   - o   Welcome God's wonderful way for abundant life.
   - o   Keep God's covenant, be faithful.
   - o   Obedience to live a better, holy life.
   - o   Remember God's amazing work.
   - o   Believe in God each day.
   - o   Trust God will provide food.
   - o   Speak well about God.
   - o   Trust in God's saving power.
   - o   Worship God with all their heart.
   - o   Remember God saved them from enemies.

   Pray for your family and friends and whoever God puts in your life to repent.

4. **Divine Wrath** - The Israelites were living in sin for quite some time, and they did not show any effort to repent from wickedness nor any desire to turn to God. Justice was served when God unleashed his divine wrath on them for idolatry and evil behavior (See Psalm 78:21-22, 30-31, 44-51, 59-67).

How did God unleash his divine wrath? Check all that apply.

- o Turned rivers to blood so they can't drink from streams
- o Sent swarms of flies to devour them
- o Sent frogs to destroy them
- o Send locusts to destroy crops and fruit of their labor
- o Sent hail, thunder, and frost to destroy vines, cattle, flocks, and sycamores
- o Sent a plague to strike people down
- o Struck down firstborns in Egypt
- o Rejected Israel
- o Left his dwelling tent at Shiloh where God dwelt with mankind
- o Gave Israel over to their enemy
- o Fire devoured young men
- o Young women had no marriage song
- o Priests fell by the sword
- o Rejected the tent of Joseph
- o Did not choose the tribe of Ephriam

Pray for your family and friends and whoever God puts in your life to repent.

77

5. **Praise God for His Good Work** - Next, identify good work God has done for the Israelites. (See Psalm 78:1-4, 12-16, 23-29, 38-39, 43, 52-55, 68-72). Praise God for the blessings He provided!

What good work did God do for his people? Check all that apply.

- o   God gave them ears to hear His teachings.
- o   He made lessons known to his people.
- o   He recorded his good work in the Bible.
- o   He performed wonders in Egypt and Zoan.
- o   He divided the Red Sea and let them pass through it.
- o   He led his people with a cloud & fiery light.
- o   He provided water from a rock.
- o   He gave the Israelites manna from heaven.
- o   He directed the south wind.
- o   He provided meat and winged birds.
- o   He gives them food they crave.
- o   He makes an atonement for their sin.
- o   He has compassion on them.
- o   He led his people out of Egypt.
- o   He brought them to a land of milk and honey.
- o   He drove out their enemies.

Thank God for his good work!

6. **Good Work People Do** - Thank God for people who let God work through their life.

   What good work did God's people do (See Psalm 78:5-7, 34-35)? Check all that apply.

   - o   They teach God's Word to their children.
   - o   They teach glorious deeds of the Lord to their children.
   - o   They do not hide God's Word from their children.
   - o   They teach divine wonders to their children.
   - o   Moses established law in Israel.
   - o   Jacob's testimony tells us about God and divine authority.
   - o   God' s people teach God's work.
   - o   They remember the law of Moses.
   - o   They know God is their rock.
   - o   They repent from sin.
   - o   They seek God earnestly.
   - o   They know God is their Most High God redeemer.
   - o   They know God chose the tribe of Judah to provide the one and only Savior.
   - o   God's people built Solomon's temple.
   - o   David served God.
   - o   David shepherded God's people.
   - o   David shepherded with an upright heart.

Below, list at least five ways God is working in your life or ways you want Him to work in your life.

Lord, help us let You do a good work in our life
and in our family's lives. Amen.

7. **Four Tips for Judging** – Here are four simple tips for effective judging as follows:

- Do not judge unless it is your duty to do so. *Above all, keep loving one another earnestly, since love covers a multitude of sins. (1 Peter 4:8)*
- Judge the behavior. It is so very important to value the person for being made in the image of God. Love the person; separate the value of the person from a bad behavior.
- God always sees the heart of the person.
- Consider your own shortcomings. God has compassion on the person who expresses godly sorrow.

If all of this "judging" seems overwhelming, Hebrews 5:14 shows us how to go about judging.

What do we need to constantly practice if we want to judge correctly?

Read Hebrews 5:14 below.

But solid food is for the mature, for those who have their powers of discernment trained by constant practice to distinguish good from evil.

Turn Hebrews 5:14 and/or four tips above into a prayer below.

8. **Govern People Well** - King Solomon asked God to help when Solomon wanted to govern the people of Israel. What did Solomon ask for?

    Read 1 Kings 3:9 below.

    Give your servant therefore an understanding mind to govern your people, that I may discern between good and evil, for who is able to govern this your great people?

9. **Solomon's Palace** – King Solomon's palace was called the House of the Forest of Lebanon. Where did he judge in his palace?

    Read 1 Kings 7:7 below.

    In addition, he built a hall for the throne, the Hall of Justice, where he was to judge. It was paneled with cedar from floor to ceiling.

    In the Supreme Court of the United States (SCOTUS), how many justices do we currently have?

    How many are conservative? How many are liberal? Do you think this matters?

DAY 3 – **Parable of the Two Gates** (a.k.a. Narrow and Wide Gates)

Throughout the Bible, we see example after example of people in every generation who need to decide between two very different ways. In the section below, underline which way is better. Meditate on the better way, affirming each one.

- Worship God or worship idols.
- Follow God's way or follow self.
- Proclaim God's name or deny God.
- Learn God's work in history or ignore it.
- Love Jesus or avoid him.
- Seek life or seek death.
- Live for God or live for self.
- Live in God's kingdom on earth or live in a destructive kingdom on earth.
- Serve God or serve false idols.
- Bless God's people or curse God's people.
- Read God's Word or ignore God's Word.
- Enter the narrow gate that leads the way to life or enter the wide gate that leads to destruction.

Dear Lord, give me wisdom to stay on the narrow path.
Give my loved ones wisdom to stay on the narrow path.
Bless all the saints who have tasted and seen that the
Lord is good to persevere on the narrow path of life.
Deliver the captives, set them free to get on the narrow
path of life. Amen.

1. **Two Options** - In the parable of the Two Gates, Jesus provided two options to choose from, either choose the narrow gate to life or the wide gate to destruction. The two gate options really are black and white; choose destruction or choose life.

   Read Matthew 7:13-14 below.

   Enter through the narrow gate. For wide is the gate and broad is the way that leads to destruction, and many enter through it. But small is the gate and narrow the way that leads to life, and only a few find it.

   \-   Jesus Christ

   From this day forward, circle which of the following ways will you choose on a daily basis:

   - Do you choose the broad way of destruction or the narrow way of life?

   - Do you choose the wide gate that leads to destruction or the narrow gate that leads to life?

   Dear Lord, please give me wisdom to discern good and evil, see the path to life, and stay on it. Give my family wisdom to discern good and evil, see the path to life, and stay on it. Amen.

2. **Three Options** - In Joshua 24:15, Joshua gave the people three options. Select God's standard for better living by circling the option you choose this day forward.

   Read Joshua 24:15 below.

   And if it is evil in your eyes to serve the LORD, choose this day whom you will serve, whether the gods your fathers served in the region beyond the Euphrates River, or the gods of the Amorites in whose land you dwell. But as for me and my house, we will serve the LORD.

Serve Ancient gods	Serve Modern gods	Serve the LORD GOD

3. **Wickedness Before the World Flood** - What kind of wickedness was found before the worldwide flood?
   Read Genesis 6:5, 11-12 below.

   The LORD saw that the wickedness of man was great in the earth, and that every intention of the thoughts of his heart was only evil continually. (Genesis 6:5)

   Now the earth was corrupt in the sight of God, and full of violence. And God looked upon the earth and saw that it was corrupt; for all living creatures on the earth had corrupted their ways. (Genesis 6:11-12)

4. **Coming of the Son of Man** - When Jesus returns, it will be like the "days of Noah" (See Matthew 24:37). Jesus instructed his disciples to be ready for his return (See Matthew 24:44). Blessed is the faithful and wise servant of Jesus because *Jesus the Master* will reward His faithful and wise servants (See Matthew 24:45-47). TIP: Leaders, do not argue about pre-trib or post-trib views. Read Scripture in context, cross reference, and pray for wisdom.

   Jesus described what it will be like immediately after the tribulation when the sign of the Son of Man appears.

   What will the return of Jesus be like? Check all that apply.

   (From Matthew 24:29-31)

   o The sun will be darkened.
   o The moon will not give its light.
   o The stars will fall from heaven.
   o The heavens will be shaken.
   o A sign of the Son of Man will appear in heaven.
   o All people on earth will mourn.
   o All people on earth will see the Son of Man coming on the clouds of heaven with power and great glory.
   o Jesus will send out his angels with a loud trumpet call.
   o The angels will gather His elect from the four winds, from one end of heaven to the other.

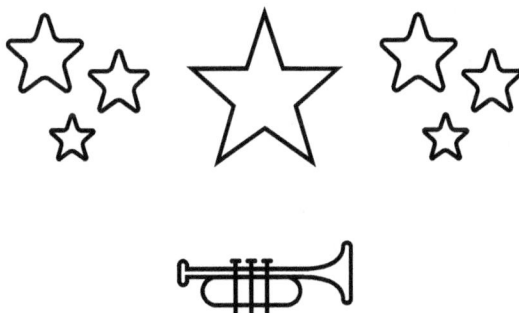

Praise God for preparing a glorious place for us!

5. **Human Heart** - Jesus warned us both good and bad can come out of the human heart. Each human person has a physical heart that beats when the physical body is alive. The *heart* is also a figure of speech for the mind and emotion connection, which includes desires, attitudes, decisions, and feelings.

Underline seven evil things that can come out of the spiritual human "heart."

Read Matthew 15:19 below.

For out of the heart come evil thoughts, murder, adultery, sexual immorality, theft, false witness, slander.

Underline nine good things that can come out of the spiritual human "heart." Read Galatians 5:22-23.

But the fruit of the Spirit is love, joy, peace, patience, kindness, goodness, faithfulness, gentleness, and self-control. Against such things there is no law.

Dear Lord,
Help us love our neighbor, spread joy wherever we go,
and choose peace over anger.
Help us show kindness, compassion, and mercy.
Help us be generous with our time and resources.
Help us remain faithful to serve YOU.
Help us to keep a tight rein on our tongue.
Help us show self-control in our words and actions.
Amen.

6. **Wide Road of Destruction** - Paul tells us the consequence of being on the wide road of destruction. What will happen?

Read Romans 1:28-32 below.
Underline all the consequences of being on the wide road of destruction.

And since they did not see fit to acknowledge God, God gave them up to a debased mind to do what ought not to be done. They were filled with all manner of unrighteousness, evil, covetousness, malice. They are full of envy, murder, strife, deceit, maliciousness. They are gossips, slanderers, haters of God, insolent, haughty, boastful, inventors of evil, disobedient to parents, foolish, faithless, heartless, ruthless. Though they know God's righteous decree that those who practice such things deserve to die, they not only do them but give approval to those who practice them.

The good news is that we can choose the narrow gate of Jesus Christ and walk on the narrow path of truth that gives life. Truth is narrow because the opposite is false.

Dear Holy Spirit,
Please help me and my family grow in love, joy, and peace.
Help us repent from all ungodliness.
Help us be patient and kind.
Transform us and let us glorify YOU.
Amen.

7. **Narrow Path of Life** - Compare how Micah and Jesus sum up the "narrow path of life."

 Read Micah 6:8 and Matthew 22:37-39 below.
 Underline traits of living on the narrow path of life, the better life.

 He has told you, O man, what is good; and what does the LORD require of you but to do justice, and to love kindness, and to walk humbly with your God?
 (Micah 6:8)

 And he said to him, "You shall love the Lord your God with all your heart and with all your soul and with all your mind. This is the great and first commandment. And a second is like it: You shall love your neighbor as yourself.
 (Matthew 22:37-39)

 Ask someone the following questions this week. How did they respond?

 What is your spiritual belief?
 To you, who is Jesus?

 Have you ever heard of the... Four Spiritual Laws (Romans Road, Three Circles, good news Gospel message, etc.)?

 Do you think there is a heaven or a hell?
 If what you believe is not true, would you want to know?

Dear Lord,
I want to honor the two greatest commandments
of loving You and loving one another.
Help me ask someone these very important questions.
Help me care about the souls of other people.
Amen.

8. **Wash Your Robe** - John explained we need to "wash our robes" to get access to the tree of life and enter the city by the gates (See Revelation 22:14). He says we are to "wash our robes in the blood of the Lamb" (See Revelation 7:14). Another figure of speech for "wash your robe" is to "clothe yourself" in God's righteousness. We "wash our robes" and "clothe ourselves" in the satisfying, redeeming work God has done for us. Just as Adam and Eve accepted the atoning work God did for them (See Gen. 3:21), we also can accept the atoning work God did for us (See John 3:16).

Practice sharing the good news Gospel message. Below, the Four Spiritual Laws is a tool you can use. You can also use tools such as the Three Circles, Romans Road, the Bridge, the Evangelism Cube, the VBS bead bracelet, the Then What? tract, the G.O.S.P.E.L. message, the 1-minute Gospel, or the 5 Finger Method.

(1) Spiritual Law #1 – GOD LOVES - God shows us His love in His Son, Jesus. Read Romans 5:8. *...but God shows his love for us in that while we were still sinners, Christ died for us.*

(2) Spiritual Law #2 – SIN SEPARATES – Read Romans 3:23. *...for all have sinned and fall short of the glory of God, and are justified by his grace as a gift, through the redemption that is in Christ Jesus.* (Why do we all need to be saved?)

(3) Spiritual Law #3 – JESUS SAVES – Read Romans 6:23. Also read John 3:16, and 2 Corinthians 5:15) *For the wages of sin is death, but the free gift of God is eternal life in Christ Jesus our Lord.* (How does the work of Jesus save us?)

(4) Spiritual Law #4 – ACCEPT CHRIST – Read Romans 10:9. *...because, if you confess with your mouth that Jesus is Lord and believe in your heart that God raised him from the dead, you will be saved.* (What must we do to be saved?)

Practice the *Four Spiritual Laws* with someone this week or next week. Ask someone, "Are you ready to accept Jesus as your personal Lord and Savior?"

9. **Abundant Life** - After a person accepts Christ as his or her personal Lord and Savior, Jesus explained we can experience abundant life on earth.

   How do believers experience abundant life? Check all that apply.

   o   We are sanctified in the truth of God's Word.
       (From John 17:17)

   o   We walk in the light.
   o   We have fellowship with one another.
   o   The blood of Jesus Christ cleanses us from all sin.
   o   We confess our sins and repent from all unrighteousness.
       (From 1 John 1:7-9)

   o   We are washed with the Word of God.
       (From Ephesians 5:26)

   o   We are washed, sanctified, and justified in the name of the Lord Jesus
       Christ and by the Spirit of God.
       (From 1 Corinthians 6:11)

   o   We are joined to the Lord and become one spirit with him. (From 1
       Corinthians 6:17)
   o   The joy of the Lord is our strength (From Nehemiah 8:10).

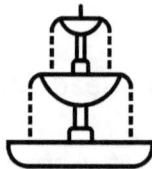

Heavenly Father,
Help me and my family remain in the Word of God.
Help us obey the Word of God.
Help us love the Word of God.
Help us show the fruit of the Holy Spirit.
Help us show mercy and compassion.
Help us be a comfort to those you put in our life.
Amen.

DAY 4 – **Parable of the House on a Rock**

(a.k.a. Two Houses, See Luke 6:46-49)

After a person receives Christ as his or her personal Savior, it is important for the person to experience abundant life on earth. Jesus gives us the *House on a Rock* parable to show us we need to survive storms if we want to experience abundant life on earth. The house built on the rock will survive a storm, but the house built on sand will not survive. The main lesson to learn is that a life built on obeying God's Word will survive all storms, but a life built elsewhere will not. Jesus pointed out we need to listen to his words and obey them.

We see a similar story in the *Three Little Pigs* by James Halliwell-Phillipps, c.1886. The house built with bricks survived, but the houses built with straw and sticks did not. The big bad wolf represents all the various storms in life, storms that try to knock us down. Upon further analysis, we also learn that hard work pays off. In both stories, the house that survives the storm has a solid foundation. Effective materials were used to build a house. Hard work went into building it.

Dear Lord, I want to build my life on obeying You. Help me and my family members build a life on hearing Your Word, following Your Word, and obeying You. Amen.

Read Matthew 7:24-27 below.

Everyone then who hears these words of mine and does them will be like a wise man who built his house on the rock. And the rain fell, and the floods came, and the winds blew and beat on that house, but it did not fall, because it had been founded on the rock. And everyone who hears these words of mine and does not do them will be like a foolish man who built his house on the sand. And the rain fell, and the floods came, and the winds blew and beat against that house, and it fell, and great was the fall of it.

1. **Meaning of House on the Rock** - Jesus tells us the meaning of the House on the Rock parable.

   What did Jesus say is the meaning? Underline two positive actions we can take.

   Read Matthew 7:24.
   Everyone then who hears these words of mine and does them will be like a wise man who built his house on the rock.

Heavenly Father,
Have mercy on me and my family.
Open our ears to hear Your Word.
Let us have self-control to follow Your instructions
For living well.
Amen.

2. **Diligent Work** - King Solomon was filled with divine wisdom. He told the story of a hardworking, diligent Ant. He observed that the ant works without anyone telling him to work. The ant finds purpose in working. The ant finds food, takes food back to a colony of ants, and helps the colony survive. (See Proverbs 6:6-8)

When the pyramids were built, 20K-100K workers worked together to get it done. It took perhaps 20 years to build a magnificent pyramid. In comparison, it took Noah about 100 years to build the ark. Have you ever built something and felt a sense of satisfaction when it was finished? If so, what was it? Give God thanks for the accomplishment.

If a believer wants to work in God's magnificent kingdom on earth, where is a good starting place? Read Colossians 3:17 and 1 Corinthians 10:31.

And whatever you do, in word or deed, do everything in the name of the Lord Jesus, giving thanks to God the Father through him.

So, whether you eat or drink, or whatever you do, do all to the glory of God.

What work are you doing in the name of the Lord Jesus for the glory of God?

3. **Cornerstone** - Churches are named *Cornerstone*. Sunday school classes are named *Cornerstone*, and we love to sing the praise and worship song, *Cornerstone*. A particular cornerstone was prophesied in Isaiah.
   Who is the Chief Cornerstone for all people?

   Read Acts 4:11-12 and 1 Peter 2:6.

   *This Jesus is the stone that was rejected by you, the builders, which has become the cornerstone. And there is **salvation** in no one else, for there is no other name under heaven given among men by which we must be saved.* (Acts 4:11-12)

   For it stands in Scripture:

   "Behold, I am laying in Zion a stone, a cornerstone chosen and precious, and whoever believes in him will not be put to shame." (1 Peter 2:6)

   ...therefore, thus says the Lord GOD, "Behold, I am the one who has laid as a foundation in Zion, a stone, a tested stone, a precious cornerstone, of a sure foundation: 'Whoever believes will not be in haste.' (Isaiah 28:16)

   Sing: Cornerstone

   My hope is built on nothing less than Jesus' blood and righteousness.

   I dare not trust the sweetest frame, but wholly trust in Jesus' name.

   In Christ alone, Cornerstone, weak made strong in the Savior's love.

   Through the storm, He is Lord, Lord of All.

4. **Waking Up** – JUST FOR FUN! Keep in mind, we all have different routines in various seasons in our lives.

Once you begin to build your life on the solid rock, Jesus Christ, you might find yourself waking up early in the morning. You have probably heard the saying, "The early bird catches the worm." The saying is not found in Scripture, but the divine precept was placed in Scripture centuries earlier. The saying was published by William Camden in the seventeenth century. Way before Camden was born, God gave us more than thirty references relating to the benefit of waking up early to get meaningful work done.

According to a research study:
- 20% of people wake up by 5:30am.
- 23% wake up between 6-6:30am.
- 26% wake up between 6:30-7:30am.
- 31% wake up after 7:30am.

How early did Jesus wake up and what did he do?

Read Mark 1:35 below.

And rising very early in the morning, while it was still dark, he departed and went out to a desolate place, and there he prayed.

Dear Heavenly Father,
I want to wake up early
and direct my prayer to You.
Help me and my family wake up early,
pray, and fellowship with You.
Amen.

5. **Divine Words of Jesus** – In the parable of the Two Houses, Jesus clearly explained how to be wise. He said to hear his words and put them into practice (See Matthew 7:24).

   When we listen to the words of Jesus, what assurance does Jesus give that his words really are God's words?

   Read John 8:28, 38 below.

   Jesus said to them, "When you have lifted up the Son of Man, then you will know that I am he, and that I do nothing on my own authority, but speak just as the Father taught me.
   (John 8:28)

   I speak of what I have seen with my Father, and you do what you have heard from your father.
   (John 8:38)

Dear Heavenly Father,
Open my ears to hear the Words of Jesus.
I want to put the Words of Jesus into practice.
Help me and my family to hear the Words of Jesus
and put them into practice.
Let us hear Your Words.
Amen.

6. **Great Storm at Sea** – From time to time, we might go through a storm when it seems like Jesus is not paying attention. Matthew recorded a true story of a great storm at sea. Jesus had been sleeping on a boat while the storm raged. When his disciples on the boat woke Jesus, they pleaded with him. "Save us, Lord; we are perishing!"

How did Jesus respond to his disciples while the storm was raging? And how did Jesus respond to the great storm? Notice what Jesus said and did.

Read Matthew 8:26-27.

And he said to them, "Why are you afraid, O you of little faith?" Then he rose and rebuked the winds and the sea, and there was a great calm. And the men marveled, saying, "What sort of man is this, that even winds and sea obey him?" (Matthew 8:26-27)

Dear Lord,
I want to have the kind of faith
that You are pleased with.
Help me and my family members
to have great faith in You.
Help us not be afraid of the wind.
Help us not be afraid of the storm.
Help us stay calm and focused on you
and your provision.
Amen.

7. **Remain Steadfast** – We will all go through various storms in life. We will face difficult situations beyond our control. Below are a few verses that equip us for those difficult times. These verses give us hope and help us put our faith in God.

Slowly meditate on the verses below.
Turn them into affirmations.

Rejoice in hope, be patient in tribulation, be constant in prayer. Romans 12:12

Blessed is the man who remains steadfast under trial, for when he has stood the test he will receive the crown of life, which God has promised to those who love him. James 1:12

I can do all things through Christ who strengthens me.
Philippians 4:13

But Jesus looked at them and said, "With man this is impossible, but with God all things are possible." Matthew 19:26

Many are the afflictions of the righteous, but the LORD delivers him out of them all.
Psalm 34:19

8. **Prepare for Jesus to Return** – In the parable about the Ten Maidens, Jesus gave us simple instructions for a community of believers to be prepared and watchful for the Second Coming of Christ (See Matthew 25:1-13). No one knows the day except for our Heavenly Father (See Matthew 24:36).

What is the way we can be prepared -and have assurance of salvation – for the Second Coming of Christ? Check all that apply.

- o Listen to the words of Jesus.
- o Believe Jesus was sent by God.
  (John 5:24)
- o Repent from sin.
- o Be baptized in the name of Jesus Christ.
  (Acts 2:38)
- o Believe Jesus died for all our sins.
- o Believe Jesus was buried and rose from the dead. (1 Corinthians 15:3-4)
- o Proclaim the gospel message.
  (Mark 16:15)
- o Believe by faith you are a son or daughter of God in Christ Jesus our Lord.
  (Galatians 3:26)

When Jesus returns to earth, will everyone see him? (See Revelation 1:7.)

Heavenly Father,
Help me and my family
To be ready for when
Jesus returns
And judges the world.
Amen.

DAY 5 – New Wine Parable

In the Bible, we find divine covenants in the Old Testament and divine covenants in the New Testament. A divine covenant is a divine promise established by the Lord God Almighty. The purpose of establishing divine covenants throughout history is for mankind to know God, call on His name, praise Him, give Him thanks, and live in a good relationship with Him.

After the fall in the Garden of Eden, God provided a covering (i.e. an atonement) for their sin. What covering did God give Adam and Eve?

> *"And the Lord God made for Adam and for his wife garments of skins and clothed them."*
> (Genesis 3:21)

God has provided an atonement for our sin by giving us the Lamb of God, Jesus Christ, who forgives us of all our sins and gives us power over sin.

The New Wine parable shows us that Jesus made an atonement for our sin to give us life. Today, we can still call upon the name of the Lord God Almighty, receive divine grace, and experience a personal relationship with Him. God created you so that you can enjoy life with Him forever. Amen!

What does Jesus, the Lamb of God, do for us?
List at least four things.

Session Three: Parables

From the days of Moses until the 3-year ministry of Jesus Christ, a *priest* called on the name of the Lord God Almighty for the people. A Levitical priest worked in the temple, performing temple duties (See Hebrews 9:1-6). A Levitical High Priest would enter the holy of holies room once a year, asking God to forgive them of all their sins (Hebrews 9:7). In the Bible, we have numerous records of priests and prophets, and some of those people were both. A *prophet* is someone who hears the Word of God and relates it to the people. Today, every born-again believer has inherited a royal priesthood (1 Peter 2:5) and redemption through the blood of Jesus (Hebrews 9:11-15). Christ followers are a kingdom of priests (Revelation 5:10). Now we will journey through the Old Testament, remember several godly priests who called upon the name of the Lord, and learn about divine covenants.

On the chronological list below, circle the names of people who were operating under the Levitical priesthood. Yes, it is important to understand the history of a royal priesthood. Then discuss if Adam, Noah, and Melchizedek were royal priests.

- Adam, Eve, and Enosh

- Noah

- Melchizedek

- Abraham, Isaac, Jacob, & Joseph

- Moses, Aaron

- Samuel, King David

- Elijah, Elisha

- Daniel

- Jesus the new covenant (new wine)

- A Royal Priesthood

1. **Call on the Name of the Lord** - Enosh was born when Adam was about 230 years old. Enosh was Adam's grandson. During the days of Enosh, people began to call upon the name of the Lord. Are you calling the name of the Lord?

   Read Genesis 4:25-26 below.

   And Adam knew his wife again, and she bore a son and called his name Seth, for she said, "God has appointed for me another offspring instead of Abel, for Cain killed him." To Seth also a son was born, and he called his name Enosh. **At that time people began to call upon the name of the LORD.**

   Today, when people call upon the name of the Lord, who does God give riches to?

   Read Romans 10:12-13.

   Paul explained, "For there is no distinction between Jew and Greek; for the same Lord is Lord of all, bestowing his riches on all who call on him. For 'everyone who calls on the name of the Lord will be saved.'"

   Song: *I Will Call Upon the Lord*
   Lyrics:
   I will call upon the Lord, for He is worthy to be praised. (2x)
   So shall I be saved from my enemies.
   The Lord liveth, blessed be the Rock, and let the Rock of my salvation be exalted.

2. **Everlasting Covenant After the Flood** - After the flood, the population narrowed down to eight people: Noah, Noah's wife, Noah's three sons named Shem, Ham, and Japheth, and Noah's three daughters-in-law (See Genesis 8:18). Noah built an altar to the Lord and offered burnt offerings on the altar. Then God made an everlasting covenant.

Read Genesis 8:21-22 below.

And when the LORD smelled the pleasing aroma, the LORD said in his heart, "I will never again curse the ground because of man, for the intention of man's heart is evil from his youth. Neither will I ever again strike down every living creature as I have done. While the earth remains, seedtime and harvest, cold and heat, summer and winter, day and night, shall not cease."

What promises did God make? List at least three divine promises.

The rainbow is the sign of an everlasting covenant. What does the rainbow represent?

(See Genesis 9:13-16)

3. **Melchizedek** – Before the Levite priests were ever appointed, a priest named Melchizedek blessed Abram. This is the first time in the book of Genesis we see a person who is called a *priest of the God Most High*.

Read Genesis 14:18-20 below.

And Melchizedek king of Salem brought out bread and wine. (He was priest of God Most High.) And he blessed him and said,

"Blessed be Abram by God Most High,
Possessor of heaven and earth;
and blessed be God Most High,
who has delivered your enemies into your hand!"

And Abram gave him a tenth of everything."

What did Melchizedek give to Abram?

What blessing did Melchizedek give to Abram?

What did Abram give to Melchizedek, the king of Salem?
(Note: Salem is a city later called Jerusalem)

Note: Melchizedek was not a Levite. Levite priests began later with Abraham's great grandson, Levi, and the descendants of Levi.

4. **Abraham Built Altars and Called Upon the Lord** - Abram built an altar to the Lord in Moreh and another one between Bethel and Ai (See Gen. 12:7-8). Abraham received significant promises from God.

    The Lord led Abraham to a mountain in the land of Moriah where Abraham built an altar for his son, Isaac. An angel of the Lord called to Abraham two times. The first time, the angel told him, *"Do not lay your hand on the boy or do anything to him, for now I know that you fear God, seeing you have not withheld your son, your only son, from me"* (Gen. 22:12).

    The second time the angel called to Abraham, the angel promised numerous descendants, including offspring that will bless all the nations. The angel told Abraham why a divine blessing was given to him.

Read Genesis 22:18 below.

   ...and in your offspring shall all the nations of the earth be blessed - because you have obeyed my voice.

What did the angel say to Abraham?

First Time

Second Time

Later, Isaac and his servants continued to call upon the Lord. The Lord told Isaac why he was receiving a blessing. Underline what the Lord promised to Isaac.

Read Genesis 26:23-25 below.

And the LORD *appeared to him (Isaac) the same night and said, "I am the God of Abraham your father. Fear not, for I am with you and will bless you and multiply your offspring for my servant Abraham's sake."*

So Isaac built an altar there and called upon the name of the LORD *and pitched his tent there. And there Isaac's servants dug a well.*

Abraham's name was made into a great nation through his offspring, including his grandson, Jacob, whose name was changed to Israel. The days of Abraham, his son Isaac, and Isaac's son, Jacob, occurred approximately from 2100 BC to 1800 BC, which is called the Patriarchal Period. We see the "old wine covenant" operating through Melchizedek, confirm to Abraham, and expand with Jacob's twelve sons. Later, the covenant thrived during the life of Moses and continued to increase during King Solomon's temple. From Abraham to the resurrection of Jesus, the span is about 2,000 years.

What promise did the Lord give to Isaac?

5. **Levite Priests** - In about 1440 BC, God worked through Moses to lead the Israelites out of Egypt so they could freely call upon the name of the Lord. After the Ten Plagues and crossing the Red Sea on dry ground, Moses and the people of Israel sang a song to the Lord (See Exodus 15). After they left Egypt, the Israelites needed water in the wilderness of Shur. Moses cried out to the Lord. Then Moses threw a log into bitter water, and the water became sweet (Genesis 15:25).

   Underline four things God told the Levite priests and the people of Israel to do. Circle the divine promise. Read Exodus 15:26 below.
   Check all that apply.

   > *If you will diligently listen to the voice of the LORD your God, and do that which is right in his eyes, and give ear to his commandments and keep all his statutes, I will put none of the diseases on you that I put on the Egyptians, for I am the LORD, your healer.*

   o   Diligently listen to the voice of the Lord your God.
   o   Do what is right in God's eyes.
   o   Listen to God's commandments.
   o   Keep God's commandments.

   Moses and his brother Aaron were from the tribe of Levi (See Exodus 6:16-20). During the life of Moses, the Levite priests were Aaron and his sons.

   What four things did God instruct Moses to do for the priests?
   Read Exodus 28:41 below.

   > *And you shall put them on Aaron your brother, and on his sons with him, and shall anoint them and ordain them and consecrate them, that they may serve me as priests.*

A leader of priests doesn't just lead. A leader of priests SERVES and EQUIPS God's people, i.e. the body of Christ, to go do kingdom work.
It is worth it to obey divine guidelines.

6. **Samuel the Prophet and Priest** - The Lord God Almighty gave more than 600 commandments for successful living to Moses and the Israelites. God worked through Moses and Joshua so they could transport the Israelites back to the land God promised. After the Israelites returned to the land of milk and honey, where previously Melchizedek was priest of the Most High God, we learn that God eventually raised up Samuel and later, King David. Samuel was a prophet, Judge, and Levite Priest.

As a prophet, what did Samuel instruct the house of Israel to do?
Check all that apply. Read 1 Samuel 7:3-4 below.

And Samuel said to all the house of Israel, "If you are returning to the LORD with all your heart, then put away the foreign gods and the Ashtaroth from among you and direct your heart to the LORD and serve him only, and he will deliver you out of the hand of the Philistines." So the people of Israel put away the Baals and the Ashtaroth, and they served the LORD only.

- ○ Return to the Lord with all your heart.
- ○ Put away foreign gods.
- ○ Put away Ashtaroth (goddess worship).
- ○ Direct your heart to the Lord.
- ○ Serve the Lord only.

As a priest, what did Samuel do at Mizpah when calling upon the name of the Lord? Check all that apply. (Read 1 Samuel 7:5-11)

- ○ Prayed to the Lord for the Israelites.
- ○ Drew water and poured it out before the Lord.
- ○ Fasted on that day.
- ○ Offered a lamb as a burnt offering.
- ○ Cried out to the Lord for Israel.

7. **Elijah's Contest with False Prophets** - After King David, false prophets of Baal started to become a significant problem during Elijah's time. Today, we see a similar problem with false teachers and false doctrine. It is important to answer, Who is the true God?

What contest did Elijah propose and carry out?

Read 1 Kings 18:24a below.

And you (prophets of Baal) call upon the name of your god (Baal), and I (Elijah) will call upon the name of the LORD, and the God who answers by fire, he is God.

Describe what happened after Elijah called upon the name of the Lord.

Then the fire of the LORD fell and consumed the burnt offering and the wood and the stones and the dust, and licked up the water that was in the trench. And when all the people saw it, they fell on their faces and said, "The LORD (YAHWEH), he is God; the LORD (YAHWEH), he is God."

8. **Jesus, the Great High Priest** - The author of Hebrews explained that Jesus is the Great High Priest in the order of Melchizedek. Both Jesus and Melchizedek were not from the tribe of Levi. All the priests before Jacob were not Levites (See Hebrews 5:6, 5:6-20, 7:1-11). As the Greatest High Priest, Jesus entered the holy of holies and secured an eternal redemption. His unblemished blood purifies our conscience from dead works to serve the living God (See Hebrews 9:11-14).

   Jesus is from the genealogy of Jacob, but not from Jacob's son, Levi. Which son of Jacob is Jesus from? (Read Matthew 1:1-2)

   Abraham was the father of Isaac, and Isaac the father of Jacob, and Jacob the father of Judah and his brothers…

   In addition, see the prophecy in Genesis 49:10 (also Revelation 5:5).

8 Judah, your brothers shall praise you;
your hand shall be on the neck of your enemies;
your father's sons shall bow down before you.
9 Judah is a lion's cub;
from the prey, my son, you have gone up.
He stooped down; he crouched as a lion
and as a lioness; who dares rouse him?

10 The scepter shall not depart from Judah,
nor the ruler's staff from between his feet,
until tribute comes to him;
and to him shall be the obedience of the peoples.
11 Binding his foal to the vine
and his donkey's colt to the choice vine,
he has washed his garments in wine
and his vesture in the blood of grapes.
12 His eyes are darker than wine,
and his teeth whiter than milk.

9. **New Covenant** – Jesus is the Greatest High Priest who ministers to born-again believers who are the royal priesthood. The main purpose of Jesus's 3-year ministry was to present the New Covenant to a royal priesthood.
Read Hebrews 8:6-7 below.

> *But as it is, Christ has obtained a ministry that is as much more excellent than the old as the covenant he mediates is better, since it is enacted on better promises. For if that first covenant had been faultless, there would have been no occasion to look for a second (ESV). See New Living Translation (NLT).*

Jesus said he didn't come to abolish the law. Rather, he came to fulfill the law (See Matthew 5:17). Nevertheless, in doing so, the author of Hebrews explained that Jesus made the Old Covenant obsolete (See Hebrews 8:13). Jesus is the final sacrifice, once for all, who made an atonement for all our sin.

What is the new covenant prophesied by Jeremiah 31:33-34?
Check all that apply.

- ○ God will put his law in the minds of his people.
- ○ God will write his laws on their hearts.
- ○ The Lord will be their God.
- ○ They will be His people.
- ○ All believers will know God.
- ○ God will remember our sins no more.
  (See Hebrews 8:10-12)

What does Peter tell the royal priesthood to proclaim?
Read 1 Peter 2:9 below.

But you are a chosen race, a royal priesthood, a holy nation, a people for his own possession, that you may proclaim the excellencies of him who called you out of darkness into his marvelous light.

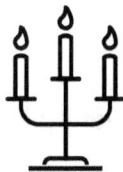

10. **New Wine, the New Way** - Jesus explained that new wine cannot be placed into old wineskins. If someone tries to place new wine in old wineskins, then the pressure of the gas from the fermentation would break the skin and the wine would be lost. New wine must be placed in new wineskins.

Read the New Wine Parable from Matthew 9:17 below.

> *Neither is new wine put into old wineskins. If it is, the skins burst and the wine is spilled and the skins are destroyed. But new wine is put into fresh wineskins, and so both are preserved.*

The *old wine* represents the old way of living with Levitical priesthood rituals, both scriptural and traditional, and other old traditions of the Hebrews that are not described in Scripture. For example, John the Baptist's disciples might have been fasting twice a week as a tradition, but fasting twice a week is not a commandment. (See the context in Mathew 9:14-17.)

Old Way

New Way

New wine represents the new way of accepting Jesus as the Lamb of God, the Savior of the world who takes away our sin. The new wine is the better way of knowing God's presence and power in the life of Jesus Christ. Jesus is the "once for all" perfect sacrifice that makes animal sacrificing no longer necessary. The new wineskins are people today who know the beauty of God's presence in the Father, Son, and Holy Spirit. The new wine centers on the gospel of Christ because it is the power of God for salvation to everyone who believes, both Jews and Gentiles. (See Romans 1:16)

DAY 6 - **Put on the whole Armor of God**

PERSONAL APPLICATION - The sword of the Spirit is the Word of God. Please keep in mind, some people are comfortable sharing personal things, but others are not. We are to use the Word of God, not twist it (See Ephesians 6:10-20).

1. In the parables of Jesus, is there a sin to avoid? If so, what is it?

Matthew 5:15

Do not hide the Light of God in your life.

2. Is there a divine promise to trust? If so, what is it?

Galatians 5:22-23

The Holy Spirit will help me express the fruit of the spirit.

3. Is there a command to obey? If so, what is it?

See Day 3, Abundant Life. Turn to page 90. The Joy of the Lord is a result.

4. What does the New Wine parable say about God's character, his nature, or his work?

    Read John 3:16 as a prayer below.

Pray for five people - one at a time - and fill their name in the blank.

LORD God, Your word says You love _____.

You have given Your one and only Son, Jesus, to _____.

Please help _____ believe in Jesus as

his/her Savior. Your word promises that _____

shall not perish but have eternal life for believing in YOU.

5. What do the parables of Jesus say about mankind? What do we need to let the parables of Jesus do in our life?

    Read 2 Timothy 3:16 as a prayer below.

LORD God, your Word says all Scripture is breathed out by YOU.

Your Word is profitable for teaching, for reproof, for correction, and

for training in righteousness, that the man of God

_____ may be complete, equipped for

every good work.

6. How have believers set a good example for us to follow? Check all that apply.

   o   We get to know God's character
   o   Get to know His works
   o   Listen to the Word of God
   o   Learn his guidelines for living an abundant life
   o   Find grace, walk in grace
   o   We ask for wisdom
   o   Enjoy peace in His presence
   o   Praise Him for being good
   o   Give Him thanks
   o   Give Him all the glory
   o   Magnify Him
   o   Experience divine blessings

7. Read Psalm 42 for comfort.

8. What verse can I meditate on?
   Psalm 42:11

   Why are you cast down, O my soul,
   and why are you in turmoil within me?
   Hope in God; for I shall again praise him,
   my salvation and my God.

9. Practice using the parables to encourage someone else.

    o   The parables of Jesus teach us about the kingdom of heaven on earth.
    o   They fulfill Old Testament prophecy.
    o   They show us his authority.
    o   They reveal truth to sincere hearts.

10. What truth is the Holy Spirit teaching in the parables of Jesus? Let it be our prayer.

    o   Be the salt of the earth.
    o   Let your light shine.
    o   Choose the narrow path that leads to life.
    o   Build your house on obeying Jesus Christ.
    o   Give thanks for our Great High Priest, Jesus.
    o   Give thanks for inheriting a royal priesthood.
    o   Proclaim the good work God has done.
    o   Praise God for making an atonement for us.
    o   Be ready for Jesus to return.
    o   Praise God for giving us eternal life.

Who can you invite to church? Pray for them by name.
Who can you invite to Bible study? Pray for them by name.
Who can you bring to Jesus? Pray for them by name.

Chapter 4

JOHN THE BAPTIST

(Matthew 3 & 11)

*People went out to John the Baptist
from Jerusalem and all Judea
and the whole region around the Jordan.
Confessing their sins,
they were baptized by him
in the Jordan River.*
Matthew 3:5-6

Green Leafed Tree by Water

In this chapter, we will see the role of John the Baptist as one of the most important people in history. Jesus said, *"Truly I tell you, among those born of women there has risen no one greater than John the Baptist. Yet even the least in the kingdom of heaven is greater than he"* (Matthew 11:11). John the Baptist prepared the way for Jesus Christ the Messiah, performed water baptisms, called people to repent from sin, and directed his disciples to Jesus.

Jesus explained the "kingdom of heaven on earth" is in our midst.
See Luke 17:20-37 for a glimpse of the divine kingdom on earth that is to come. Read Romans 14:17 below for a glimpse of the divine kingdom on earth right now.

> *For the kingdom of God is not a matter of eating and drinking but of righteousness and peace and joy in the Holy Spirit.*

- DAY 1 - Ministry of John the Baptist
(Matthew 3:1-12)

- DAY 2 - Old Testament Washings
(Exodus 19 & 30)

- DAY 3 – John, a Friend of the Bridegroom
(Matthew 11:1-6)

- DAY 4 - Water Baptism of John & Fire Baptism of Jesus
(Matthew 11:20-24)

- DAY 5 – Kingdom of Heaven on Earth
(Matthew 11:25-30)

DAY 1 - Ministry of John the Baptist

In Luke 1:5-25, we learn about John the Baptist's mom and dad, Elizabeth and Zechariah. John's parents were righteous, walked blamelessly, had no children, and were advanced in years. One day when Zechariah was in the temple burning incense as a Levite priest, an angel named Gabriel appeared to him. Gabriel prophesied to Zechariah that he and Elizabeth would have a son and name him John.

1. **Gabriel Prophesied to Zechariah**

Read Luke 1:16-17 below.

And he (John) will turn many of the children of Israel to the Lord their God, and he will go before him in the spirit and power of Elijah, to turn the hearts of the fathers to the children, and the disobedient to the wisdom of the just, to make ready for the Lord a people prepared.

What did the angel Gabriel prophesy John would do?

2. **Prepare the Way** - John the Baptist fulfilled prophecy. He prepared the way for the Messiah, Jesus Christ. Here's how: John was the one who baptized people in the Jordan River, and he called people to be ready for the Messiah's arrival. (Read Matthew 3:1-12)

   Read Matthew 3:1-2 below, then compare it with Isaiah 40:3. The prophet Isaiah prophesied about 700 years earlier than the time of John the Baptist.

   In those days John the Baptist came preaching in the wilderness of Judea, "Repent, for the kingdom of heaven is at hand." For this is he who was spoken of by the prophet Isaiah when he said,

   > *"The voice of one crying in the wilderness:*
   > *'Prepare the way of the Lord; make his paths straight'"* (Matthew 3:1-2).

   A voice of one calling: "Prepare the way for the LORD in the wilderness; make a straight highway for our God in the desert. (Isaiah 40:3)

   How did John the Baptist prepare the way for the Messiah?

   Read Mark 1:4-8 below.
   John appeared, baptizing in the wilderness and proclaiming a baptism of repentance for the forgiveness of sins. And all the country of Judea and all Jerusalem were going out to him and were being baptized by him in the river Jordan, confessing their sins. Now John was clothed with camel's hair and wore a leather belt around his waist and ate locusts and wild honey. And he preached, saying, "After me comes he who is mightier than I, the strap of whose sandals I am not worthy to stoop down and untie. I have baptized you with water, but he will baptize you with the Holy Spirit."

3. **Turn Away from Bad Behavior** – In the Old Testament, we find a mandate for people to wash and cleanse as they prepared to encounter God's presence (See Exodus 19:10-11). The priests were commanded to wash with water in preparation for their services in the temple (See Exodus 29:4).

    John was gifted from birth and filled with the Holy Spirit in his mother's womb. Elizabeth and Zachariah knew about John's calling to *prepare the way*, and John knew about his calling to prepare the way (See Luke 1:15). They were all looking forward to John who would prepare the way for the Messiah. Out in the wilderness, John called people to be ready for the Messiah. He called everyone to repent from sin, which means to turn away from ungodly, unholy behavior. Spiritual repentance is when a person turns away from ungodly, unholy behavior and turns toward God for a cleansing from all ungodliness and all unholiness. God is the one who determines what is holy and godly. He is the one who fills us with His Holy Spirit each day when we draw near to Him. For example, King David expressed a prayer of repentance. David knew God as the one who spiritually washes us from all our sin. Water is a symbol for spiritual renewal. Water can clean dirt off our physical body, but God's Holy Spirit cleanses our heart from all unholiness. Read Psalm 51:2 below and see how King David looked to God for spiritual renewal.

    > *Wash me thoroughly from my iniquity,*
    > *and cleanse me from my sin!* (Psalm 51:2).

    > *Purge me with hyssop, and I shall be clean;*
    > *wash me, and I shall be whiter than snow.*
    > (Psalm 51:7)

What kind of baptism did John do?

Read Matthew 3:11a below.

I baptize you with water for repentance.

4. **Jesus's Baptism** - What kind of baptism did John say Jesus would do? Read Matthew 3:11b below.

He (Jesus) will baptize you with the Holy Spirit and fire.

Simply put, fire symbolizes the Holy Spirit who purifies our heart. God is described in Hebrews 12:29 as a consuming fire. Malachi explained God is like a refiner's fire who refines gold and silver.

When we offer (present) our life to God (See Romans 12:1 below), what did Malachi say we need to do before we work in ministry?

Read Romans 12:1 below.

I appeal to you therefore, brothers, by the mercies of God, to present your bodies as a living sacrifice, holy and acceptable to God, which is your spiritual worship.

Read Malachi 3:2-3 below.

But who can endure the day of His coming? And who can stand when He appears? For He will be like a refiner's fire, like a launderer's soap. And He will sit as a refiner and purifier of silver; He will purify the sons of Levi and refine them like gold and silver.

Then they will present offerings to the LORD in righteousness.

Pray for you and your family and your enemies to do the following:
- o Turn away from all ungodliness and unholiness.
- o Worship the one true God.
- o Let the one true God purify their heart.
- o Do kingdom work.

5. **Voice from Heaven** – Immediately after John baptized Jesus, a voice from heaven spoke, identifying the nature of Jesus. Read Matthew 3:16-17 below.

> *And when Jesus was baptized, immediately he went up from the water, and behold, the heavens were opened to him, and he saw the Spirit of God descending like a dove and coming to rest on him; and behold, a voice from heaven said, "This is my beloved Son, with whom I am well pleased."*

Matthew quoted Isaiah 42:1 to further explain the ministry of Jesus as it fulfills prophecy from Isaiah. Jesus proclaimed justice as the Lamb of God.

Read Matthew 12:18 below.
> *Behold, my servant whom I have chosen, my beloved with whom my soul is well pleased. I will put my Spirit upon him, and he will proclaim justice (judgement) to the Gentiles.*

In the book of Luke, we learn another parable that Jesus taught, the *Parable of the Persistent Widow*. According to Jesus, how do salty saints get justice?

Read Luke 18:1, 7-8 below.
> *And he told them a parable to the effect that they ought always to pray and not lose heart…*
>
> *Jesus said, "And will not God give justice to his elect, who cry to him day and night? Will he delay long over them? I tell you, he will give justice to them speedily. Nevertheless, when the Son of Man comes, will he find faith on earth?"*

Dear Heavenly Father, help me draw near to you day and night.
Help my loved ones find salvation in Jesus as Lord and Savior.
Thank you for your grace we find in Jesus. I pray that when
Jesus returns to earth, He will find great faith in his people.
Amen.

6. **Wheat and Chaff Parable** - John the Baptist gave a parable, *Wheat and Chaff*, to describe the nature of good and evil existing together temporarily. In the future, evil will be separated from good. Today, we see the same concern about evil existing in the world. Sometimes bad things happen to good people because 1.) We temporarily live in a fallen world. 2.) Sometimes trials and tribulations test our faith to make it stronger. 3.) God's sovereign will is for wheat and chaff to live together for now. 4.) Our faith journey is a witness to those around us. Compare John's parable to the parable of Jesus.

Read John's parable from Matthew 3:12 below.

His winnowing fork is in his hand, and he will clear his threshing floor and gather his wheat into the barn, but the chaff he will burn with unquenchable fire.

Read Jesus's parable from Matthew 13:24-30 below.

Let both grow together until the harvest, and at harvest time I will tell the reapers, "Gather the weeds first and bind them in bundles to be burned, but gather the wheat into my barn."

What happens to good and evil in the end? Explain what John and Jesus taught about good and evil.

Keep praying for five of your loved ones, neighbors, and enemies to hear the good news Gospel message. Write their first name below and pray for their salvation. If they are already saved, pray for their sanctification.

DAY 2 – Old Testament Washings

1. **Consecration at Mount Sinai** – The Lord instructed Moses to have the people consecrate themselves, wash their garments, and be ready for the Lord to give Moses instructions. God gave Moses details for the tabernacle furnishings, the Ten Commandments, and all the rules given at Mount Sinai (See Exodus 19:10, 14).

   Why were the people instructed to consecrate and wash?
   Click all that apply.

   - To be God's treasured possession
   - To be a kingdom of priests
   - To be a holy nation
   - To hear God speak to Moses
   - To believe Moses
   - To meet God at the foot of the mountain
   - To see the Lord come down to the top of the mountain
   - To tremble before the Lord
   - To fear the Lord
   - To be cleansed from sin
   - To see God talk to Moses from heaven
   - To remember God's name

Dear Heavenly Father,
Thank you for water that washes our body and keeps us hydrated.
Thank you for the Holy Spirit who purifies our heart from all ungodliness.
Thank you for the Word of God that transforms our mind.
Amen.

2. **Bronze Basin** - The Lord instructed Moses to place a Bronze Basin in the Tent of Meeting (Tabernacle) for washings where priests could get clean before presenting a food offering to the Lord. Whenever Aaron and his sons entered the Tent of Meeting or approached the alter to minister, they were required to wash their hands and clean their feet (See Exodus 30:17-21).

Later, King Solomon provided a new and improved version of the temple. A Bronze Basin was provided for priests to use for washings. It was circular; 15 feet wide from rim to rim, 7.5 feet deep, and a base of 45 feet in circumference, holding more than 10,000 gallons of water, a pool called Molten Sea. Ten basins were also provided for the priests to rinse and wash. (See 2 Chronicles 4:1-6, 1 Kings 7:23-26)

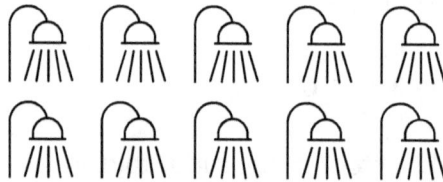

The purpose of the Bronze Basin is significant.
Read Exodus 30:21 below.

They shall wash their hands and their feet, so that they may not die. It shall be a statute forever to them, even to him and to his offspring throughout their generations.

In Matthew 15:119, Jesus explained what defiles a person.

For out of the heart come evil thoughts, murder, adultery, sexual immorality, theft, false witness, slander. These are what defile a person. But to eat with unwashed hands does not defile anyone.

Explain the difference between the following:
- Wash your hands (before you handle food, after you wipe a runny nose).
- Let the Word of God purify your heart.
- Discuss a dirty heart vs a dirty body.

3. **Priestly Purification** – Moses was instructed by the Lord to cleanse the Levite priests. The purification included washing, cleansing, and sprinkling water on the priests. Today, we wash with soap and water to cleanse our physical body from germs and prevent infectious disease. Yes, we still need to wash our hands before we prepare food and after we use the restroom.

At a military recruit training command center in Illinois, new recruits were told to wash their hands at least five times a day. After two years, those recruits had 45% fewer cases of respiratory illness than the previous recruits. The program was called Operation Stop Cough.

Compare the Old Covenant purification from Numbers 8:5-7 with the New Covenant purification mentioned in Hebrews 10:22. Are they similar?

Explain how water purification differs from a spiritual purification.

> *And the LORD spoke to Moses, saying, "Take the Levites from among the people of Israel and cleanse them. Thus, you shall do to them to cleanse them: sprinkle the water of purification upon them, and let them go with a razor over all their body, and wash their clothes and cleanse themselves."* (Numbers 8:5-7)

> *...let us draw near with a true heart in full assurance of faith, with our hearts sprinkled clean from an evil conscience and our bodies washed with pure water.*
> (Hebrews 10:22)

4. **Steadfast Love** - In Hosea 6, we hear the prophet calling people to return to the Lord so they could find refreshment like rain.

Read Hosea 6:3 below.

Let us acknowledge the Lord. Let us press on to acknowledge him. As surely as the sun rises, he will appear. He will come to us like the winter rains, like the spring rains that water the earth.

In Hosea chapter 6, Hosea described some of the problems in Israel. Click all that apply.

○   Their love disappeared
○   Outward rituals without love
○   Evil behavior and wicked schemes
○   Bloodshed and murder
○   Attacking victims
○   Prostitution and defilement
○   Broke the covenant
○   Unfaithful to God

Hosea encouraged people to pray and ask God to forgive them.
Read Hosea 14: 2 below.

Forgive all our sins
and receive us graciously,
that we may offer the fruit of our lips.

Jesus gave us a special revelation about "streams of living water" being the Holy Spirit (See John 7:37-39). He explained how to receive streams of living water. How do we receive streams of living water flowing within?

Read John 7:38 below.

Whoever believes in me (Jesus), as the Scripture has said, 'Out of his heart will flow rivers of living water.'

5. **Water Purification** – We find several different signs of divine covenants in the Old Testament. These signs include water purification, animal sacrifice, circumcision, the sabbath rest, and the rainbow. Water purification was used for various purposes such as cleansing for personal hygiene, consecrating priests, and preparing for worship. Baptism is a symbol for getting right with God, washing away a person's sin, and preparing for ministry.

Discuss the greater purpose for each Old Testament symbol.

OLD TESTAMENT SYMBOL	GREATER PURPOSE
Water purification	Cleanse from sin, prepare for ministry
Animal sacrifice	Atonement for sin, burnt offerings
Circumcision	Cut sin out, get rid of wickedness
Sabbath rest	Spiritual renewal, rest & honor God
Rainbow	Redeeming mercy

Baptism is a symbol of the Holy Spirit who washes, regenerates, and renews the inner person.

Did Jesus baptize with water?

- o   Yes
- o   No
- o   Yes, but no

Read John 4:1-3 below.
Now when Jesus learned that the Pharisees had heard that Jesus was making and baptizing more disciples than John (although Jesus himself did not baptize, but only his disciples), he left Judea and departed again for Galilee.

DAY 3 – John, a Friend of the Bridegroom

1. **Increase and Decrease** - John the Baptist knew that Jesus is the promised Messiah who takes away the sins of the world. He introduced Jesus as the Lamb of God to all the people. John assured his disciples that Jesus is the promised Messiah. Jesus fulfills messianic prophecy, performs miracles, changes people's lives for the better, teaches with authority, ministers to a royal priesthood, and gives abundant life. John introduced Jesus as the Lamb of God who forgives sins, which fulfills messianic prophecy.

   Disciples of John the Baptist were concerned that all the people were going to Jesus and Jesus's disciples to get baptized instead of getting baptized by John the Baptist.

   How did John respond?

   Read John 3:30 below.

   He (Jesus) must increase, but I (John) must decrease.

   In your life, who must increase? Who must decrease? How is that done?

   INCREASE

   DECEASE

2. **Lead Them to Jesus** - The day came when both John the Baptist and Jesus were baptizing in separate locations. Disciples of John were concerned that Jesus was baptizing more people than John the Baptist. Then John explained what was supposed to happen (See John 3:22-36).

> *John answered, "You yourselves know how plainly I told you, 'I am not the Christ, but I have been sent before him.' The one who has the bride is the bridegroom. The friend of the bridegroom, who stands and hears him, rejoices greatly at the bridegroom's voice. Therefore, this joy of mine is now complete. He must increase, but I must decrease."*
> (John 3:28-30)

>> BRIDE = people getting a water baptism; the church
>> BRIDEGROOM = Jesus
>> FRIEND OF THE BRIDEGROOM = John

John explained that Jesus must increase. He also explained that he, John the Baptist, must decrease. We, too, need to point others to Jesus. If we don't, then we are increasing ourselves instead of increasing Jesus. John the Baptist faithfully carried out his ministry to prepare the way for the Messiah and point others to Jesus.

John, the Beloved Disciple of Jesus, gave us a strong reason to believe Jesus as the Messiah.
Read John 20:31 below.

> *...but these are written so that you may believe that Jesus is the Christ, the Son of God, and that by believing you may have life in his name.*

Practice telling someone. "It's worth it to believe Jesus is your personal Savior because it's the way we find eternal life, true life, and abundant life on earth."

3. **Give Them Assurance** - Herod Antipas put John the Baptist in prison because John condemned Herod for marrying Herodias, his half-brother Philip's wife (See Mark 6:17, Matthew 14:3-5).

While in prison, John sent his disciples to ask Jesus a question. "Jesus, are you the one who is to come, or shall we look for another?" Today, we still see all different kinds of people who ask the same question, "Is Jesus the Christ (the prophesied Messiah)?" Jesus helped the disciples of John the Baptist understand how to know Jesus is the Messiah. What assurance did Jesus give John's disciples?

Read Matthew 11:4-5 below.

And Jesus answered them, "Go and tell John what you hear and see: the blind receive their sight and the lame walk, lepers are cleansed and the deaf hear, and the dead are raised up, and the poor have good news preached to them. And blessed is the one who is not offended by me."

Practice telling someone the following:
- Jesus gave sight to the blind.
- He healed people who couldn't walk.
- He healed lepers.
- He healed deaf people.
- He raised the dead.
- He preached good news to the poor.
- He fulfilled prophecy.
- He gave us the Sermon on the Mount.
- He taught about the kingdom on earth.
- He blesses those who are not offended by his teaching.
- He gives us peace.
- He gives us joy.
- He gives us love.
- He is preparing an eternal place for us.
- He will return to judge evil.
- He is the first fruit of a resurrected life.
- He gives us the hope of eternal life in heaven.

4. **Bring Others to Jesus** - John the Baptist understood he was called by God to prepare the way for the Messiah. John saw the Holy Spirit descend from heaven like a dove and remain on Jesus when John the Baptist baptized Jesus. John the Baptist knew for sure that Jesus is the one who baptizes others with the Holy Spirit. John the Baptist proclaimed that Jesus is the Lamb of God who takes away the sin of the world.

Read John 1:29 below.
> *The next day he (John) saw Jesus coming toward him, and said, "Behold, the Lamb of God, who takes away the sin of the world!"*

At that time, Andrew was a disciple of John the Baptist, but Andrew left John to go follow the Lamb of God, Jesus (See John 1:40). Therefore, John did his job by directing his disciples, including Andrew, to follow Jesus. Who did Andrew bring to Jesus?

Read John 1:42.
> *Andrew brought him to Jesus. Jesus looked at him and said, "You are Simon the son of John. You shall be called Cephas" (which means Peter).*

Like Andrew, we can bring people to Jesus.

John prepared the way for the Messiah. Discuss how we can prepare the way for the second coming of Christ. Discuss how we can point others to Jesus.

5. **John's Answer to Isaac** - About twenty centuries earlier, a young boy asked his dad, "Where is the lamb for a burnt offering?"

Read Gen. 22:7-8 below.
  And Isaac said to his father Abraham, "My father!"

  And he (Abraham) said, "Here I am, my son."

  He (Isaac) said, "Behold, the fire and the wood, but where is the lamb for a burnt offering?"

  Abraham said, "God will provide for himself the lamb for a burnt offering, my son."

  So, they went both of them together.

How did John the Baptist answer Isaac twenty centuries later?

Read John 1:29 below.

  The next day he (John the Baptist) saw Jesus coming toward him, and said, "Behold, the Lamb of God, who takes away the sin of the world!"

Practice telling someone that Jesus is the Lamb of God who takes away the sin of the world. Now explain what the Lamb of God means.

6. **Glory to the Lamb and to Him Who Sits on the Throne** - In Revelation 5, we find out the Lion of the Tribe of Judah has conquered as the Lamb of God. We see the Lamb is the only one worthy to judge and redeem mankind. In response, the twenty-four elders and four living creatures sing a new song. (See Revelation 5:1-8)

What do the elders and living creature sing?
Read Revelation 5:9-10. Check all that apply.

   o   Worthy is the Lamb to open the scroll and its seven seals.
   o   Worthy is the Lamb who was slain.
   o   The Lamb's blood saves people from every tribe, language, and nation.
   o   The Lamb made a kingdom of priests to God to reign on earth.

How can you respond with John the Baptist and with every creature in heaven and earth and under the earth and in the sea?

Read Revelation 5:13b.
"To him who sits on the throne and to the Lamb be blessing and honor and glory and might forever and ever!"

Sing: Holy Forever

A thousand generations falling down in worship,
To sing the song of ages to the Lamb.
And all who've gone before us,
And all who will believe will sing the song of ages to the Lamb.
Your name is the highest, Your name is the greatest.
Your name stand above them all.
All thrones and dominions,
All powers and positions,
Your name stands above them all.
And the angels cry, "Holy!"
All creation cries, "Holy!"
You are lifted high! Holy forever!

DAY 4 – Fire Baptism of Jesus

1. **Believe Jesus** –John baptized with water and fulfilled prophecy as the one who prepared the way for the Lord. He prepared the way for the Messiah, Jesus Christ.

   What did John the Baptist instruct people when he baptized them in water? Read Acts 19:4 below.

   > *Then Paul said, "John verily baptized with the baptism of repentance, saying unto the people, that they should believe on him which should come after him, that is, on Christ Jesus."*

2. **The Mighty One** - John the Baptist proclaimed that "Jesus will baptize with the Holy Spirit and fire" whereas John the Baptist baptized with water for repentance and pointed his disciples to Jesus.
   (See Matthew 3:11, Luke 3:16)

   John decreased himself, and he increased Jesus. How did John "increase Jesus"?

   > *John said, "I indeed baptize you with water unto repentance: but he that cometh after me is mightier than I, whose shoes I am not worthy to carry. Jesus shall baptize you with the Holy Spirit, and with fire."*

3. **Empowered for Kingdom Work** – A water baptism is a public declaration that a person repents from sin and is cleansed from all sin in the name of the Father, Son, and Holy Spirit. It is a symbol of repenting from sin and receiving Jesus as his or her personal Lord and Savior who made an atonement for all sins. Water is a symbol that God purifies a person from all unrighteousness.

John the Baptist clearly explained to his disciples that one mightier than he would be baptizing with Holy Spirit fire. Jesus baptizes with the Holy Spirit, empowering his disciples to proclaim the word of God with power.

What does the gift of the Holy Spirit do to believers?
Read Acts 4:31 below.
And when they had prayed, the place in which they were gathered together was shaken, and they were all filled with the Holy Spirit and continued to speak the word of God with boldness.

Dear Heavenly Father,
Thank you for filling me with the Holy Spirit each day.
Thank you for purifying me with the Holy Spirit to speak the
Word of God with boldness and see You heal others. Amen.

4. **Joel's Prophecy Fulfilled** - In Acts 2:14-21, Peter affirmed that the pouring out of the Holy Spirit on all people is a fulfillment of Joel's prophecy in 2:28-29.

Joel prophesied that God will pour out the Holy Spirit on all people.

Read Joel 2:28-29 below.
And it shall come to pass afterward,
that I will pour out my Spirit on all flesh;
your sons and your daughters shall prophesy,
your old men shall dream dreams,
and your young men shall see visions.
Even on the male and female servants
in those days I will pour out my Spirit.

Peter declared the fulfillment of Joel's prophesy.
Read Acts 2:17 below.
And in the last days it shall be, God declares,
that I will pour out my Spirit on all flesh,
and your sons and your daughters shall prophesy,
and your young men shall see visions,
and your old men shall dream dreams…

List some of the results of God pouring out his Holy Spirit on all people.

5. **Washing from the Holy Spirit** – John the Baptist knew Jesus would be baptizing with Holy Spirit "fire" whereas John baptized with water as a personal, public declaration for repentance, turning away from sin and turning toward God our Heavenly Father (See Matthew 3:11, Mark 1:4-8). John understood that Jesus is the Lamb of God who purifies our heart. John used the word *fire* to explain the work of the Holy Spirit that purifies us from all unrighteousness through Jesus. In 1 John 3:3 below, underline what happens when we hope in Jesus as our personal Lamb of God who takes away our sin.

What happens when we put our hope in Jesus?

Read 1 John 3:3 below.
And everyone who thus hopes in him (Jesus) purifies himself as he (Jesus) is pure.

How did God save us?

Read Titus 3:4-7 below.
But when the goodness and loving kindness of God our Savior appeared, he saved us, not because of works done by us in righteousness, but according to his own mercy, by the washing of regeneration and renewal of the Holy Spirit, whom he poured out on us richly through Jesus Christ our Savior, so that being justified by his grace we might become heirs according to the hope of eternal life.

Discuss the difference between being purified and getting saved.

What is the difference between sanctification and justification?

6. **Empowered for a Purpose** – God calls everyone today to repent from sin and place faith in Jesus as Lord and Savior for salvation. Today, water baptism is a sign that a person repents from sin and has proclaimed personal faith in Jesus. The main purpose of receiving special power from the Holy Spirit is to go be a bold witness for Jesus and proclaim the Gospel message.

Read Acts 1:8 below.
But you will receive power when the Holy Spirit has come upon you, and you will be my witnesses in Jerusalem and in all Judea and Samaria, and to the end of the earth.

When the disciples of Jesus were gathered in one place, the day of Pentecost arrived when the disciples were filled with the Holy Spirit. Immediately, Peter began preaching the Gospel of Jesus Christ.

Read Acts 2:36 below.
Peter said, "Let all the house of Israel therefore know for certain that God has made him both Lord and Christ, this Jesus whom you crucified."

What did Peter instruct the disciples of Jesus Christ to do?

Read Acts 2:38 below.
And Peter said to them, "Repent and be baptized every one of you in the name of Jesus Christ for the forgiveness of your sins, and you will receive the gift of the Holy Spirit."

- Practice telling someone, "God has made Jesus both Lord and Messiah. Jesus is the Savior of the whole world."

- Practice asking someone, "Have you been baptized with water in the name of Jesus Christ as a public declaration of Jesus forgiving you of all your sins?"

- Thank God for your baptism, for forgiving you of all your sins, and for receiving the gift of the Holy Spirit.

7. **New Life in Christ** - The water baptism of John differs from the fire baptism of Jesus. Water is a symbol for God cleansing us from sin. Fire is a symbol for Jesus purifying us from all sin, once for all, for giving us power over sin, and for giving us the ability to do kingdom work. Explain the difference between water baptism and fire baptism.

What actions followed first century Pentecost and water baptism?
Read Acts 2:42-47.
Check all that apply.

- o   Believers were devoted to the first century apostle teaching.
- o   Believers were devoted to fellowship.
- o   Believers were devoted to breaking bread together.
- o   Believers were devoted to praying together.
- o   Awe came upon every soul.
- o   Many wonders were done through apostles.
- o   Believers helped anyone who was in need.
- o   They attended the temple together.
- o   They received food with glad hearts.
- o   They praised God for having favor with all people.
- o   The Lord added to their number day by day.

Have you been baptized by water and received the gift of the Holy Spirit, empowered for kingdom work? If not, ask your pastor to baptize you with water in the name of the Father, Son, and Holy Spirit.

DAY 5 – Kingdom of Heaven on Earth

John the Baptist proclaimed, "Repent, for the kingdom of heaven is at hand" (Matthew 3:2). Jesus also told his twelve disciples to proclaim the kingdom of heaven is at hand (Matthew 10:7).

1. Son of the Living God

Once you get to know the nature of who Jesus is as your personal Savior, your Greatest High Priest (Intercessor), your Lion of Judah (Most Powerful King), and your Immanuel (God with us), there is increasing joy in sharing the good news message. Jesus asked his disciples a very important question: *Who do people say the Son of Man is?*

And they said, "Some say John the Baptist, others say Elijah, and others Jeremiah or one of the prophets."
(Matthew 16:14)

Simon Peter had been traveling with Jesus for quite some time. Who did Simon Peter say he knew Jesus to be?

Simon Peter answered, "You are the Christ, the Son of the living God."
(Matthew 16:16)

- Is Jesus your personal Savior?
- Is He your Intercessor?
- Is He your Most Powerful King?
- Is He always with you?
- Is Jesus the Son of God?
- Is Jesus your Lord?

Practice sharing the good news message: Jesus gives us eternal life.

God has done amazing work in the life, death, and resurrection of Jesus Christ the Son of God. God gave us Jesus to teach us how to live in the kingdom on earth. God gave us grace in Jesus who paid the penalty for all our sin and gives us power over sin. God gave us Jesus as a "firstfruit" to show us we will all be resurrected. People who accept Jesus as Lord and Savior will inherit eternal life.

2. **Possibly or Certainly** – There is a big difference between believing Jesus is possibly the Messiah or believing Jesus is certainly the Messiah.

    Compare a Samaritan woman's proclamation of the nature of Jesus with John the Baptist's proclamation of the nature of Jesus.

    At the well, a Samaritan woman decided at first that Jesus was a prophet. Then Jesus told her he was the Messiah. "Jesus said to her, "I who speak to you am he" (John 4:26). The woman walked away to town, asking the people in town to consider if Jesus could be the Messiah. She motivated people to seek Jesus.

    Read John 4:29-30 below.
    Come, see a man who told me all that I ever did. Can this be the Christ (Messiah)? They went out of the town and were coming to him (Jesus).

    John the Baptist was born to prepare the way for the Messiah. He introduced Jesus as the Lamb of God who takes away the sin of the world (a.k.a. the Messiah).

    Discuss the powerful results of two different approaches:
    - Like the Samaritan woman, ask people to consider if Jesus is who he says he is, the prophesied Messiah, the Savior of the world.
    - Like John the Baptist, proclaim Jesus is certainly the Lamb of God, Messiah, and Savior of the world.

    "I'm ready to accept Jesus as a great moral teacher, but I don't accept His claim to be God." That is the one thing we must not say. A man who was merely a man and said the sort of things Jesus said would not be a great moral teacher … You must make your choice. Either this man was, and is, the Son of God: or else a madman or something worse. You can shut Him up for a fool … or you can fall at His feet and call Him Lord and God. But let us not come with any patronizing nonsense about His being a great human teacher. He has not left that open to us. (See John 1:14)

    C.S. Lewis, *Mere Christianity*

3. **Paul, a Faithful Witness** - John the Baptist was faithful to introduce Jesus as the Lamb of God who takes away the sin of the world. John was bold, urgent, and direct with everyone who drew near. John was faithful to carry out kingdom work by calling people to repent from sin and be baptized with water. John also directed his disciples to Jesus who baptizes with the Holy Spirit. Apostle Paul is another good example of someone who was faithful to proclaim the nature of Jesus Christ. Today, we can proclaim, "Jesus saves!"

In Corinth, what good news Gospel message did Paul proclaim?
Read 1 Corinthians 15:3-5 below.

> *For I delivered to you as of first importance what I also received: that Christ died for our sins in accordance with the Scriptures, that he was buried, that he was raised on the third day in accordance with the Scriptures, and that he appeared to Cephas, then to the twelve.*

If you have not yet accepted Christ as your personal Savior, say a prayer now.

> Dear Heavenly Father, I turn away from all ungodliness, and I open my heart to You. I give every part of my life to You. I receive Jesus now and forever as my personal Savior. I believe Jesus willingly died on the cross for all my sins. Thank you for forgiving me of all my sins and for giving me eternal life. I believe Jesus rose from the dead on the third day. Fill me now with your Holy Spirit. Fill me each day with a fresh filling of your Holy Spirit to do kingdom work. Help me be salt of the earth. Let Your Light shine through me. Give me discipline and wisdom to remain in Your Word. Let my kingdom work help others draw near to you. I pray for others to find grace just as I have found grace in a personal relationship with the Father, Son, and Holy Spirit. Provide a way for me to get a water baptism as a public proclamation of my new life with You. Thank you for giving me power over sin in a daily relationship with you. Thank you for giving me peace. Thank you for giving me grace.
> In Jesus name, Amen.

4. **Get Baptized** - A person can try many times to turn away from bad behavior, but when a person turns to Jesus and receives Jesus as his or her personal Savior, the person is truly cleansed and new life is found. The Lamb of God gives us new life and power over sin.

> Read Matthew 28:18-20 below.
> *And Jesus came and said to them, "All authority in heaven and on earth has been given to me. Go therefore and make disciples of all nations, baptizing them in the name of the Father and of the Son and of the Holy Spirit, teaching them to observe all that I have commanded you. And behold, I am with you always, to the end of the age."*

Water baptism is a public declaration of turning away from unrighteousness and turning to Jesus for His righteousness. It's a symbol of new life in Christ.

> *Therefore, if anyone is in Christ, he is a new creation.*
> *The old has passed away; behold, the new has come.*
>   (2 Corinthians 5:17)

> Discuss the problems of life without Christ.

> Discuss the benefits of life with Christ.

Jesus is the one and only who has power to transform us into the image of God. In the story of *The Voyage of the Dawn Treader* by C.S. Lewis, Eustace described what it was like letting Aslan the Lion peel away Eustace's dragon scales. Eustace tried to peel the scales off himself, but he couldn't get all of them off. He let Aslan peel off all the dragon scales, and then Eustace experienced great joy, swimming in water where he received his new, better skin.

5. **Gifts for Kingdom Work** - John the Baptist was called to baptize people with water and prepare the way for the Lord. Paul was called to preach the Gospel message. Some are called to baptize others with water while others are called to preach the good news Gospel message. (See 1 Corinthians 1:17)

Whatever spiritual gifts you have been given, it is important you use them to build up the kingdom on earth. Let Jesus increase in your life.

Paul listed some of the gifts in 1 Corinthians 12:4-11, Romans 12:6-8.
- Wise Words
- Knowledge in skill
- Faith
- Healing
- Miracle Works
- Prophecy
- Discern Spirits
- Tongues
- Interpretation of Tongues
- Service
- Teaching
- Exhortation
- Generosity
- Leadership
- Mercy

Discuss areas where you have served in kingdom work on earth.
- Live righteously, blameless like Job.
- Teach the Word of God, share the good news.
- Serve meals.
- Use your skills to bless others.
- Visit people in the hospital.
- Financially support a kingdom building ministry.
- Celebrate the true meaning of Christmas.
- Provide a home Bible study group.
- Serve in Vacation Bible School.
- Donate clothes and other goods.
- Reach out to neighbors with love.
- Invite people to church.
- (See Hebrews 13:16, Matthew 5:16)

6. **Malachi's Prophecy** - Jesus was familiar with Malachi's prophecy of a messenger who would prepare a way for the Messiah. Jesus told his disciples that John the Baptist fulfilled a prophecy in the book of Malachi.

Read Malachi 3:1 below.
> *"Behold, I send My messenger, and he will prepare the way before Me. Then the Lord whom you seek will suddenly come to His temple; and the Messenger of the covenant in whom you delight-- behold, He is coming," says the LORD of Hosts.*

How does Matthew 11:10 fulfill Malachi 3:1?

Read Matthew 11:10 below.
> *This is he (John the Baptist) of whom it is written, "Behold, I send my messenger before your face, who will prepare your way before you."*

John the Baptist = the messenger who prepared the way for the Messiah

Jesus = the Messenger of the New Covenant

Practice telling someone how Jesus fulfilled Messianic prophecy.

- Jesus lived in perfect obedience. He was tempted like we are, but He never sinned.
- Jesus healed the sick and blind. He freed those who were oppressed.
- Jesus taught us, using parables, about the kingdom on earth.
- Jesus is the seed who crushed the serpent's head.
- Of the kingdom of Jesus, there is no end.
- Jesus is a descendant of King David.
- Jesus gave good news to those who would listen.
- Jesus is the Lamb of God and the Lion of the Tribe of Judah.
- Jesus is the Bread of Life.
- Jesus gives eternal life to all who believe and call on Him.
- Jesus rose from the dead.
- Jesus gives us the gift of the Holy Spirit.

DAY 6 - Put on the whole Armor of God

PERSONAL APPLICATION - The sword of the Spirit is the Word of God. Please keep in mind, some people are comfortable sharing personal things, but others are not. We are to use the Word of God, not misuse it (Ephesians 6:10-20).

1. John the Baptist and Jesus both instruct us to repent, to turn away from sin. What kind of bad behavior and evil thoughts are they talking about?

Mark 7:21-23, Galatians 5:19-21, Romans 1:26-27

Evil thoughts, wickedness
Sexual immorality, sensuality, orgies, homosexuality
Theft, deceit
Murder, fits of anger, enmity, strife, rivalries
Adultery, Coveting
Envy, jealousy
Slander, divisions
Pride
Foolishness, drunkenness
Idolatry
Sorcery
Other:

2. Is there a divine promise to trust? If so, what is it?

    Acts 2:38

    And Peter said to them, "Repent and be baptized every one of you in the name of Jesus Christ for the forgiveness of your sins, and you will receive the gift of the Holy Spirit."

3. Is there a command to obey? If so, what is it?

    Acts 2:38

    And Peter said to them, "Repent and be baptized every one of you in the name of Jesus Christ for the forgiveness of your sins, and you will receive the gift of the Holy Spirit."

4. What does the ministry of John the Baptist say about God's character, his nature, or his work?

5. What does the ministry of John the Baptist say about mankind?

6. How has John the Baptist set a good example for us to follow?

   Psalm 32:5

   > *I acknowledged my sin to you,*
   > *and I did not cover my iniquity;*
   > *I said, "I will confess my transgressions to the LORD,"*
   > *and you forgave the iniquity of my sin.*

7. Read Psalm 40:2-3 for comfort.

   He drew me up from the pit of destruction,
   out of the miry bog,
   and set my feet upon a rock,
   making my steps secure.
   He put a new song in my mouth,
   a song of praise to our God.
   Many will see and fear,
   and put their trust in the LORD.

   Psalm 130:3-4
   If you, O LORD, *should mark iniquities,*
   O Lord, who could stand?
   But with you there is forgiveness,
   that you may be feared.

8. What verse can I meditate on?

   Psalm 103:12
   As far as the east is from the west,
   so far does he remove our transgressions from us.

Who can you invite to church? Pray for them by name.
Who can you invite to Bible study? Pray for them by name.
Who can you bring to Jesus? Pray for them by name.

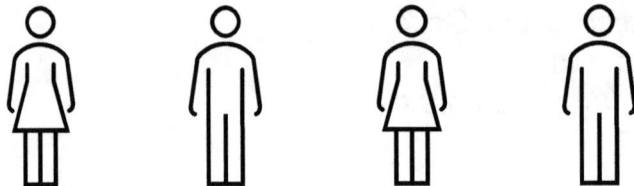